"This book presents a unique perspective on how to know you are called to do more. It reveals that there are no excuses; you have been made aware of what is needing to be done. Ask the Lord to send you. Lord, Send Me, Amen! Let's Go!"

— Chris Gifford, Founder of Thread Pull, Podcast Host of Revealing Greatness

"For twenty years I have known Evans Duren, first as a college student leader and later as a trusted friend. Consistently, Evans has striven to integrate his faith seamlessly through his family, personal life, and professional life. Anyone seeking to better live into their faith within a professional setting will enjoy and benefit from reading *Send Me*!"

— Dr. Bill McDonald, Retired Higher Education Administrator

"The reader can see themselves against the landscape of God's grace, mercy, and His Word and the tension between fear, insecurity, and faith. Evans challenges all of us to partner with God to fulfill His plan of spreading the gospel on the earth. I highly recommend this book as a must-read for all who want to know where he or she fits in God's plan."

— DR. KAREN PHILLIPS, PASTOR
AT CHRIST CENTRAL MINISTRIES,
INC.

"Evans Duren illuminates a burning topic that has many working Christians in a considerable tug-of-war. His transparency, vulnerability, and lengthy personal journey will have you aspiring to hear God's call and once and for all say 'YES' to the life God has designed you for. I highly recommend *Send Me* as a must-read for every professional."

— DAVE CARROLL, BUSINESS
COACH AT CANTILLON

"Through *Send Me* and the vision God has laid on Evan's heart, there will be a great kingdom impact because of Evan's faithfulness, God will move."

— John Crabtree, M.A.
Intercultural Studies from
Columbia International
University

Send Me

Discovering Your Mission Through Work

Evans Duren

Here an I,

Send Me.

— Evans Du

STREAMLINE
BOOKS

SEND ME

Discovering Your Mission Through Work

Cover Design by Will Severns

KUNG FONT by FGD Goodies for Designers

Streamline Books | www.WriteMyBooks.com

Paperback ISBN: 9-798-3889-1889-5

Hardcover ISBN: 9-798-3905-3068-9

April 27th, 2023

This book is dedicated to every follower of Jesus searching to bridge the gap between their faith and their work. I pray you will discover the mission God has reserved for you through your vocation.

This book is also dedicated to every person who doesn't yet have a relationship with Jesus. I pray we as believers will share the gospel in a manner that points to the true character of God through our faith and work.

Contents

As We're Going

Romans 10:13-15

"For 'everyone who calls on the name of the Lord will be saved.' How then will they call on him in whom they have not believed? And how are they to believe in him of whom they have never heard? And how are they to hear without someone preaching? And how are they to preach unless they are sent? As it is written, 'How beautiful are the feet of those who preach the good news!'"

Introduction

For as long as I can remember, I have felt a tension between my work and my faith.

As a young man, I considered studying Christian education but chose a business degree instead. I remember speaking with my father about it while driving our 1994 green Honda Accord on the backroads of South Carolina. I was on my way to the small town of Union to pick up a fraternity brother before heading to Nashville for a conference. Talking with my father as I drove, I let him know that I needed to declare a major and was leaning toward Christian education. In our discussion, my father told me he believed I should study business, and so I did.

My father and I have a phenomenal relationship. I've always valued his opinion and have often followed his advice. I graduated with a business's degree and moved into a Fortune 15 sales role shortly thereafter. It wasn't until eighteen years later that I revisited that "what do I study" conversation with him.

As I continued to wrestle with the tension, I eventually asked him why he encouraged me to study business. Why did he answer with anything other than "whatever you want to do" or "whatever makes you happy, son?" I was a little angry and felt some regret that I didn't choose the other option. I worried that the reason I continued to feel the tension may be because I had made the wrong decision.

As we spoke, my father's response removed a massive weight I had been carrying. Even though it took me several more years to fully understand the significance of his reply, it was a gift that has allowed me to further explore the divide between work and faith.

He explained that when we spoke about sales or anything business related while I was in high school, I would sort of light up and he could see an underlying excitement. As my father, he saw me in a way no one else could. Because of his own experiences and watching me grow over the years, he encouraged me to study business and pursue a career in sales. That encouragement has led me to this point in time where I finally see how to relieve the tension between work and faith.

My visions of living in a foreign country as a missionary or working for a local church were replaced with sales campaigns, quotas, and thousands of client interactions across multiple states. There have been many times I have chased money, prestige, and the advancement of my career. Even so, God has always found ways to pull me into the tension and back towards Him when I begin to live for myself rather than to serve others.

I can tell you about my first big sale, the first commission check I ever received, and standing on stage winning my Fortune 15 company's Rookie of the Year Award, but I can also tell you about praying with a father whose child had a potentially fatal diagnosis, sitting with clients who were searching for purpose and meaning beyond their work, and witnessing the hardest of hearts in business turn soft as they experienced the greatness of God for the first time.

Being great in our businesses and occupations is a wonderful thing. In fact, we as believers should be excellent in all pursuits and live as if we are working for the Lord: Whatever you do, work at it with all your heart, as working for the Lord, not for human masters, since you know that you will receive an inheritance from the Lord as a reward. It is the Lord Christ you are serving (Col 3:23-24).

When we forget it is ultimately God we serve through our work, we find ourselves building lives that do not reflect our beliefs. When people see Christian men and women in the workforce that have separated their Sunday beliefs from their careers, they do not see God. Instead, they see religious people who inject enough confusion into the world to make them question God and what it means to be a Christian.

"The greatest single cause of atheism in the world today is Christians who acknowledge Jesus with their lips and then walk out the door and deny Him by their lifestyle. That is what an unbelieving world simply finds unbelievable." - Brennan Manning.

Being a Christian does not mean our lives will be perfect. We don't forget how to sin and magically start to live holy and righteous lives that earn our admittance into Heaven. We still fall short, we still sin, we still struggle, and we are far from perfect. The difference is our lives are no longer our own, and as we learn to surrender to God's will, others recognize something different in how we live in comparison to how the world tells us we should live.

I am in awe at the number of opportunities I have had to sit with customers and coworkers in order to know them better on a personal level, far beyond any business transaction. Those moments have been the most fulfilling experiences in my career. While I have absolutely enjoyed making the money, winning the awards, closing deals, and being recognized for my efforts, I have learned not to let those accomplishments determine my worth and value.

As I have grown in my career, these are no longer the things that make work meaningful. They have been replaced with a desire to live life alongside others while utilizing my unique gifts, skills, and talents to honor God and not just myself. When I make money it no longer determines my worth–instead, it allows me to feed and care for my family while also financially investing into God's Kingdom. Winning awards and closing deals still bring me a sense of accomplishment, but I have learned to treat these things as opportunities to be involved in others' lives as they are confronted with their own journeys of belief while living in the tension between work and faith.

I am called to work, and that has meant a

career in sales up to this point. There was a time I considered moving into vocational ministry. I even began taking a few seminary classes in the evenings and online. I was not able to finish an advanced degree, but that first night on campus, I learned a lesson that made it all worthwhile.

Attending Columbia International University that first evening, I found myself in a missions class with thirty students of various ages, most of whom were working in vocational ministry. I didn't know a single person before arriving, and I remember feeling anxious and out of place. Once the professor introduced himself and outlined expectations, we went around the room introducing ourselves. I remember a number of students were looking to work in churches and mission organizations after graduation. Some were fresh out of their undergraduate programs, while others were twenty years removed from college and had long since started their own families.

The gentleman in front of me introduced himself by saying he worked in business and remained unsure of why God had called him to attend seminary. I could tell he was also a little uneasy, and, oddly enough, it comforted me to know I was not the only non-church employee in the room. I introduced myself and explained that I too was still discerning God's call on my life and had spent most of my career in sales.

As the night continued, I began to feel more relaxed but still out of place. I continued feeling like an outsider until someone approached me on the way back to my car to ask more about my career. John explained that he had spent more than twenty years in youth ministry and was very excited to have me in class. I didn't understand, so I asked him why he was excited for someone with a business background to be there.

He explained that because so many people who work in full-time ministry have been there for so long, they don't always get to see beyond the walls of their church. He was excited to hear a new perspective and looking forward to a new voice from outside the traditional vocational ministry.

As much as I loved school and would like to have finished my degree, life had other plans. While living in that tension between faith and work, I told God I wanted to be a pastor, but he said "no." In all honesty, hearing "no" hurt my pride and I questioned a lot about myself. Even my conversation with John that first night of seminary couldn't keep me from feeling inadequate to share the gospel.

Even as I write this book, I still find myself

battling the voice in my head telling me I'm not qualified to speak with you about Jesus. I'm not a pastor, I don't have a theology degree, and I'd be lying if I said I am not worried about writing something that is theologically incorrect as I discuss scripture.

There's that tension again.

I know our businesses are filled with Christian men and women trying to integrate their beliefs into a system determined to keep them locked out. So I'm going to lean into this tension. I'm going to share the gospel and encourage you in your faith and work so that you will seek and discover how God is calling you to be on mission with Him.

My first hope for this book is that by reading it, your relationship with God will either be initiated or strengthened. I will share specific stories and events from my life, but they are only written as supporting material for how God intervenes and has a specific calling for each of us, regardless of our past or our occupation. From the beginning of creation, God has walked alongside everyday people to accomplish incredible things for His kingdom.

Second, I hope to use scripture and truth to bridge the gap between who you are and what you do. To close that gap, you must discover whose you are and how that changes everything! I want doors of belief and opportunity to be flung wide open so that your work and faith collide in a newfound passion to live for Jesus in a way you may never have known was possible.

Third, I long to see men, women, and young people in and out of our churches believe their lives have purpose and value as they work for God, regardless of job title. I love our pastors, missionaries, associations, and all of the amazing people God has ordained to work within traditional ministry settings. If we are going to be on mission with God as the body of Christ, then all of us must be on mission, not just those serving within the church. God sends us all to different places in different ways. It is time for us to go and work within our appointed mission fields.

Finally, you and I have a divinely appointed role to play in God's love story of redemption. We are not perfect, and we never will be in this life. Perfection is not attainable, but that is no excuse for us to not seek excellence and to exhaust our limited time in the pursuit of His will for His people. As we go forward, my hope is that when God asks if we will go as messengers to His people, we will boldly respond, "send me."

SCRIPTURE FOCUS

ISAIAH 6:7

"And he touched my
mouth and said: 'Behold,
this has touched your lips;
your guilt is taken away,
and your sin atoned for.'"

CHAPTER 1

UNCLEAN LIPS PURIFIED

A DIVINE INVITATION

To be human is to have a purposeful role in God's creation.

— CHRISTOPHER J. H. WRIGHT

One of the most honest and raw testimonies I have ever heard was from former MLB World Series champion, Darryl Strawberry. He was a guest speaker with John Maxwell at a local event I registered to attend, but I did not know Darryl would be taking the stage to share his story. I have been a Maxwell fan since I first discovered his books in college, and baseball was my first love, so imagine my excitement when I realized the two of them would be speaking together.

As Maxwell spoke, I took several pages of notes. He is a masterful storyteller and communicator, and his time on stage was one continuous conversation with the audience.

Strawberry was a stark contrast to Maxwell. The former is a professional athlete, while the latter is a professional speaker and leadership guru. Strawberry has a public history of bad decisions and Maxwell is a pastor who blends faith and business. Both took very different paths to that stage, yet the common thread was their faith in God. They found Him at different points in life under opposite circumstances, but that day, it was clear God was with them the entire time, waiting patiently as He actively sought to work through both of them.

Strawberry brought a whirlwind of emotions to the auditorium and had many attendees, including myself, fighting back tears. He shared stories of a childhood home plagued by alcoholism and abuse at the hands of his father. He spoke of his mother who never stopped praying for him, even as she lay on her deathbed fighting cancer. He explained how he had been filled with hatred and turmoil. In spite of it all, God revealed Himself and pulled Darryl out of the drugs and anger that were ruining his life.

For anyone to share so vulnerably about their past on a public stage takes courage and a faith grounded in who they are and to whom they belong. Strawberry was born to a father who hurt him, a mother who loved him, and a home that brought immense pain. His career brought accolades and fame, but it never filled the emptiness in his soul. No amount of success or drug use could fill that void: only God was sufficient.

Strawberry eventually reconnected with his father, asked for his forgiveness, and prayed the Sinner's Prayer with him only a few months before he passed. What a beautiful testimony from a man who has lived through the highest of highs and the lowest of lows in a very public manner.

Before he left the stage, Strawberry prayed over the audience. I had to wipe the tears from my eyes. I don't know how many people can say Darryl Strawberry has prayed over them, but it was a powerful experience, and it taught me a great deal about who God is and how He works in the lives of those who love Him. Regardless of titles, gifts, difficult beginnings, or poor decisions, God takes what was intended to destroy us and uses it for His good.

As we take our next steps together in this book, I share these words from Strawberry that I imagine many of you, like me, will understand:

"I'm not qualified to preach the gospel, but the one who lives inside me is."

UNCLEAN LIPS PURIFIED

Isaiah 6 is going to set the stage for this book, but I encourage you to read more about his life and work. Isaiah was an Old Testament prophet whose life predated the birth of Jesus by about seven-hundred years. In the New Testament, Isaiah is the most quoted Old Testament prophet. He was God's messenger at a very unstable point in history, delivering His word during the reign of four kings.

Read Isaiah 61:1-2 and Luke 4:16-21 to gain a firm grasp on why this is important. You will see Isaiah's prophecy of a coming savior fulfilled in Jesus seven centuries later. While teaching in the synagogue, Jesus took the scroll of Isaiah, read the prophecy, rolled the scroll up, handed it back to the attendant and said "Today this scripture is fulfilled in your hearing" (Luke 4:21).

Read Isaiah 9:6 and 11:1 for the foretelling of Jesus' birth and then read the first chapter of

Matthew—these passages convey what Christmas is all about.

Isaiah 6 tells of an encounter Isaiah had with God through a vision. As we unpack the meaning and application of the text as it relates to Isaiah's calling into prophetic work, I want to also extrapolate some of what we read in this scripture to God's calling and desire for our lives.

What is incredible about this vision, as well as Isaiah's life and ministry, is God's absolute magnificence and holiness contrasted against Isaiah's humanity and sinfulness. God in His perfection calls Isaiah in his imperfection to be His messenger. Through Isaiah's story, God demonstrates that He works through imperfect people to carry out His mission for the sake of His glory. These verses are a redemption story: God shows mercy to Isaiah as He invites him into a new relationship rather than bringing wrath and destruction.

The first verse notes the historical timeline: this vision took place in the year King Uzziah died. Although it is not clear as to whether or not Uzziah had passed at the time of Isaiah's vision, the mention of Uzziah is crucial to understanding this text. Uzziah translates to "Jehovah is Strength" and he ruled for over fifty years. At the height of his success, Uzziah entered the temple of the Lord to burn incense on the altar and was struck with leprosy. Though the end of his life is tragic and not an ideal legacy, plenty of good occurred during his reign. The fact that Uzziah is mentioned in Isaiah's retelling of his vision says much about who Uzziah was as a king.

Isaiah is timestamping his vision while reminding us how temporal our lives are in comparison to the everlasting King, our Lord, who sits high and lifted up on His throne, the train of His robe filling the temple as He appoints kings and queens. This serves as a profound reminder that while kings and kingdoms fade, God's rule is eternal.

We are then introduced to the seraphim in verses 2-3. These are angelic creatures whose name suggests they are some fiery being. They have six wings: two covering their faces, two covering their feet, and two used to fly. The seraphim provide an incredible picture of a six-winged fiery creature who serves God while not looking directly upon Him due to His glory, all the while covering their feet out of humility and respect.

The seraphim spoke with one another repeating "holy, holy, holy" in reference to God's undeniable perfection, which set Him apart from the rest of His creation. Repetition in the Bible tells the reader to pay close attention to what is being said or happening in the text, and this is one of those moments.

We continue reading that the doorposts shake and smoke fills the temple. I imagine a thunderous sound reverberating throughout the temple as smoke, signifying the presence of God, enters the room. Often these signs meant destruction and represented God's wrath in the Old Testament, which helps to explain what happens next when Isaiah finally speaks.

"Woe is me, for I am undone! Because I am a man of unclean lips, and I dwell in the midst of a people of unclean lips; For my eyes have seen the King. The LORD of hosts" (Isaiah 6:5).

Isaiah panics at the realization that he is in the presence of the Almighty God and his sinful human condition cannot stand before the holy King. In a span of seconds, Isaiah acknowledges who he is. He deserves wrath and judgment. There is nowhere to run or hide. All he can do is wait for God to act in carrying out his sentence.

But then something incredible happens: one of the seraphim takes a live coal from the altar and touches it to Isaiah's lips. Remember, the seraphim have six wings, two of which enable them to fly. Those two wings enable the seraphim to carry out the will of God, and in this case, God's will was to purify Isaiah's heart and lips so he would be prepared to take a new message to God's people.

When he thought his life was over, God showed Isaiah mercy and prepared him for a new life dedicated to serving Him.

One thing I love about the Bible is that the words and stories it contains are still applicable to our lives thousands of years later. We have unclean lips, unclean hearts, and serve too many masters, yet God still loves us and desires a relationship with each of us.

We are heirs to a kingdom, sons and daughters of the King, with an invitation to join Him on a mission to redeem the lost in a fallen world. These verses from Isaiah's vision tell a great deal of the distance sin creates between us and God, while also reminding us of the great lengths God will go to deliver grace and mercy.

As Christians, how often do we forget who we are and *whose* we are because the world we live in does not accept or acknowledge our nobility? The world would have us believe our value and worth come from the jobs we do, the titles we carry, the money we make, our status in society, our online presence, and the accumulation of possessions

This is one of the greatest lies ever told, and we

have bought into it so deeply that we do not recognize our true identity, creating distance between who we are and how we live our lives.

How can it be that someone of royal blood would not live under the umbrella of God's righteousness and sovereignty? I believe the only viable answers are they **do not know** they have an invitation to join Him, they **do not believe** there is room for them, or they **do not want** to live under God's rule.

RSVP

I remember first seeing God at work in the marketplace while standing in a customer's office in east Tennessee. I was a sales representative calling on a surgery center, only a year out of school, and still very green. I walked into the office to see the two nurses that ordered medical supplies for the practice, and what happened next changed everything I believed about faith and work.

Lauren had turned to her desk to grab a notepad with the week's supply order, and by the time she turned back around, Donna had thrown her arms around my neck and was crying on my shoulder. I was completely shocked and had no idea what to do. I looked at Lauren, and her eyes nearly popped out of her head with shock.

Through her tears, Donna confided in Lauren and me that her husband's health had taken a turn and he was now wheelchair-bound. Through her sobs, she asked if he was being punished by God for her sins and mistakes in life. All I could do was hug her back and tell her that God does not work that way, and I didn't believe for one second that God was punishing her husband for her past.

At that moment, I realized that God was in fact at work in the business world. The problem was I still didn't understand how to serve Him, or if I could serve Him through my business, even with Donna crying in my arms.

DO NOT KNOW

My experience with Donna proved I had no idea there was an invitation for me to be on mission through my work. I was in sales, and that didn't sound remotely close to being a pastor, a minister, or a missionary. I had always considered "church work" and "God's work" to be reserved for people that are much more holy and perfect than I was. That kind of work was for people like my pastor, the missionaries I have come to know, or nonprofit and church organizations doing missions work, but not someone in sales

Around that same time, I reached out to my friend and mentor who had first helped me get into the medical industry. I told him I felt like I was making money off sick people and it didn't feel right. Thankfully, he countered my argument by explaining that while some of what we sold would be to help sick patients, we also sold multiple products that detected and prevented illness.

I was looking at sales as a self-serving profession, but my mentor showed me how we were serving countless people, most of whom we would never meet, by providing their physicians and surgeons with the proper supplies and equipment to protect and heal them. Rarely did we have an opportunity to see our supplies and equipment being used, but that doesn't mean they were gathering dust on a shelf

A few years later, I was covering a territory that stretched across South Carolina. One of my customers was a family medicine practice I visited every two weeks. One afternoon, they asked for a new defibrillator. This was an odd request because they had recently bought one, and defibrillators are not routine purchases.

As we discussed it further, the office manager

informed me they had used the defibrillator on a patient in their office the week prior and wanted an additional unit. I still have no idea who that patient was, but I was told that the defibrillator extended her life long enough for family to come see her from out of town and tell her goodbye.

Donna showed me people in the business world want to know God. My mentor taught me God gives each of us unique gifts, skills, and talents to be leveraged in serving others, regardless of occupation. Selling that defibrillator taught me that even when we don't see how, God still uses our work to help others.

Do Not Believe

It is painful to witness someone not accepting their invitation to be on mission with God due to unbelief. It isn't so much that they don't believe God works through those He calls, they simply believe they are unworthy to be called into God's service. This person questions their ability to be "good enough." This person hasn't read the entire Bible, hasn't memorized the books of the Bible, and may not be able to quote scripture. They believe in God but feel that somehow they are disqualified from intimately knowing Him because they're not formally educated or serving in a church. This person feels like their past both defines and disqualifies them from an intimate relationship with God, perhaps because they have not forgiven themselves and don't think they can experience true forgiveness and love.

This has been the greatest barrier I've had to overcome in my own faith journey. For the longest time, I looked at pastors, missionaries, and other faith-based workers as the only ones God calls to evangelism and missions. I had always pictured missionaries as people who lived in third-world countries and drank coffee in public places to try to meet people and tell them about Jesus. That was such a small view of missions. I had no idea how incredible and diverse mission work truly is.

I have always struggled with the belief that God could use everyone else but not me. I was never good enough, I loved money, was afraid His will and my will would never align, and ultimately didn't believe I could be a vessel for His work.

In my unbelief, God showed up and used one of my fears to prove both His presence in my life and His desire for me to be on mission through my vocation.

I do not enjoy flying, and something about being thirty-thousand feet in the air makes me uncomfortable. I'm not sure if it's the height or the stark realization that I have zero control, but it's not my favorite way to spend my time. Coping with my anxiety during my flights has come to include plenty of prayer, conversation with the person next to me (whether or not they are interested), and singing "Highway to the Danger Zone" to myself during every single takeoff.

One night flying back from a work event in Denver, our plane flew headfirst into a terrible storm. The flight attendants handed out candy bars and tried to keep everyone calm while my seatmates and I cracked jokes to ease our minds. I sat by a couple who had been attending a different business conference that week, and at one point I told the husband to not be upset with me if I grabbed his wife's hand out of fear, to which he promptly replied, "don't get upset if I grab yours!" The three of us felt like we had accomplished something when the plane landed, and even now, I laugh when I think about how grateful I am that they sat beside me.

As we approached our gate, I realized I had missed my connecting flight from Memphis to Charlotte. The airline booked me and several other passengers into a local hotel, and when I finally got the key to my room, I opened the door to find someone else's luggage on the bed as the room's occupant made obvious use of the restroom. I quietly put it in reverse and ran downstairs to change rooms.

My flight the next morning was so early in the day that the airport was mostly vacant, and my plane held only a few passengers. In true Evans fashion, I sat next to a woman and struck up an intentional conversation with her to combat the anxiety I could already feel creeping into my mind. In a matter of minutes, our conversation progressed from small talk to discussing how she was flying to Florida for a family emergency.

There I was, five miles in the air, and God placed me next to an older woman who was on the way to say her final goodbye to her dying sister. As the conversation continued, we went deeper into their relationship, childhood, and personal beliefs about God. The woman by whom I was seated was a believer, but her sister was not. We prayed together just before landing, and I have never seen her again.

My father picked me up from the airport in Charlotte that day, and when I got into his car I couldn't help but cry. I was furious that I had missed my flight the night before, the hotel had given me a key to an already-occupied room, I had

had to confront my fear of flying yet again, and I was missing my wife and son for another night due to the bad weather in Memphis. All that had happened on the way home from a business event led me to a seat next to this grieving woman.

DO NOT WANT

As I write, I can't help but think of the parable of the prodigal son (Luke 15:11-32). The young man in this parable is one of two sons who asks his father to give him his inheritance before the proper time. His father agrees, and soon thereafter the son leaves his father's home and travels to a distant country and begins to live a very different lifestyle than the one he lived under his father's roof. The Bible bluntly states that he "squandered his wealth in wild living" (vs 13). Eventually, he spends all of his money just as a famine strikes and he must find work in order to survive. He finds a job taking care of pigs and is tempted to eat their slop due to the hunger gnawing away at his stomach.

The son concludes that surely his father's servants are eating better than he is, and he makes a decision to return home and ask his father to make him a hired servant. When the son returns, he finds his father overcome with joy, running to greet his returning son with hugs and kisses as only a parent would. The father calls for a celebration, puts his son in the finest of robes, and places a ring on his finger and shoes on his feet.

This was certainly not the homecoming the son expected. As the celebration was underway, the *other* son, who had stayed and worked his father's land and had yet to receive his inheritance, came in from the fields. When he found out his errant brother had returned and was being celebrated, the dutiful brother became furious. When his father pleaded with him to come inside, the son recounted all the grievous things his brother had done, including squandering his inheritance

The father replies, "you are always with me, and everything I have is yours. But we had to celebrate and be glad, because this brother of yours was dead and is alive again; he was lost and is found" (Luke 15:31-32).

The prodigal son decided he did not want a seat at his father's table or to live under the umbrella of his family name, but no matter where he ran or what he did, he was still his father's son. His position within the family remained vacant, awaiting his return. Once he squandered everything he had been given and had reached the lowest point of his life, he longed for that seat at his father's table. In the middle of a pig sty, he experienced unbelief and became convinced that he would not be forgiven and accepted back into his father's home. Finally, the prodigal son did not know the love his father had for him in spite of all he had done. The choice to leave and not believe were his, but his father ultimately determined whether or not the son would be welcomed back to his birthright. The son did not know his father reserved his position because it was not a position he had earned; it was a gift given to him through none of his own efforts.

This is also how it is with God, our Heavenly Father. He has reserved for each of us who believe in Him a position within His Kingdom that we cannot purchase or somehow earn through our own good works. When we don't fully know or understand, it is still there. When we don't believe God could ever use us for His purpose, it is still there. When we run, hide, and believe we want something else rather than to sit at the King's table because we view it as a burden or a weight we can't carry, it is still there.

If we are truly honest with ourselves, I think a little bit of the Prodigal Son lives in all of us. We may not live a life that mirrors the specific ways in which he rebelled against his father, but we face our own journeys of not knowing, unbelief, and a desire to run away from our seat at God's table. The Bible is filled with stories like the Prodigal Son where God's people travel their own unique journey to the King's table, and we are no different. Just as the father of the prodigal possessed ultimate authority over his son's seat at his table, so God possesses ultimate authority over His children.

Reflection

IT IS ABUNDANTLY CLEAR THAT GOD CALLS people with countless imperfections into His service, to be on mission with Him. Even when we can't comprehend how or why God would use us as His hands and feet, we can be assured that He will purify our hearts and prepare us for the assignment ahead, just as He did with Isaiah. When we stray or find ourselves questioning our seat at the Lord's table, the prodigal son shows us that the shame we believe is too much to overcome is often no more than an illusion.

It is time for you to accept your invitation to be on mission with God. It is time to find a desire to see the world's lost be found. Believe that God has a purpose for your life that is greater than your past and bigger than your worst mistakes. He is big enough to work in and through you even though you feel unworthy and incapable. He purifies unclean lips, and I hope you will run towards His purpose for your life, refusing to turn away from the mission He has planted in your heart.

God wants you to be a kingdom builder, and is preparing you "for such a time as this."

Scripture Focus

Esther 4:14

"For if you keep silent at this time, relief and deliverance will rise for the Jews from another place, but you and your father's house will perish. And who knows whether you have not come to the kingdom for such a time as this?"

CHAPTER 2

FOR SUCH A TIME AS THIS

KINGDOM BUILDING PURPOSE

God is not in the career-building or dream-fulfilling business. God is in the kingdom-building business.

— DAVID A.R. WHITE

I don't remember the first time we spoke, but I do remember the day she walked into a pre-calculus class wiping tears from her eyes. Having to take a pre-calculus class is plenty of reason for tears, but Jamye was crying over a high school parking lot breakup. She continued wiping her eyes as she settled into her seat, which was directly in front of me. This seating arrangement was well-suited for teenage flirting, which was fortuitous because this girl was absolutely stunning.

I asked her what was wrong, and after she told me about the breakup, I quickly responded with something to the effect of "what an idiot!", in reference to the other guy. I also silently screamed "Yes!" while holding back from doing a touchdown dance up and down the aisles of our class. Though my flirting was probably not as cool in the moment as I thought it was, it is no exaggeration to say that everything in my life changed that day when this beautiful girl in my pre-calculus class smiled at me through her tears.

Since that day, we have been together for over twenty years and recently celebrated seventeen years of marriage. Those teenage feelings have turned into a love deeper than anything I could have ever imagined. Jamye somehow becomes even more beautiful as she ages, and I am continually falling further in love with her mind and heart.

Jamye's favorite piece of scripture comes from Esther 4:14. I have heard her speak "for such a time as this" over the lives of our friends and family on several occasions. While I knew there was power in that verse, I had never considered Esther's possible connection to the work and call of marketplace professionals. Jamye said it again recently as I began to write, and I suddenly began to see the connection.

There is a greater purpose in our work than we often realize. If God is the King and we are His heirs, then we are to be kingdom builders. We have the responsibility for the advancement and protection of His kingdom. The key decision point for each of us is not whether or not we will pursue kingdom building, but whose kingdom is being built by the labor of our lives.

IF I PERISH, I PERISH

Esther is the only book in the Bible that does not mention God's name, and yet He is actively working in her story of courage and calling.

Esther arrives in the palace of King Ahasuerus as a beautiful young woman to be included in his harem, along with the King's other servants and wives, and finds favor that eventually places her on the queen's throne. She goes from an orphaned girl living with her uncle to a queen in less than a year.

In the text, we learn that one of the King's high-ranking officials, Haman, develops a true hatred for Esther's uncle, Mordecai. Haman believes Mordecai has wronged him, and so in retaliation, Haman manipulates the King into signing a decree that will not only destroy Mordecai but will also destroy the Jewish people. Esther and Mordecai are both Jews, and their lives are in danger. As the story unfolds, we find in Esther 4:14 that Esther's favor with the King may be the only way to save everyone—including herself.

However, there is one small problem. In the opening chapters, the King has signed a decree that could further put Esther in mortal danger. If she were to call on the king to plead for her people without being summoned, she could be put to death. Faced with the decision to speak or remain silent, she chooses to approach him, fearlessly stating, "and if I perish, I perish" (Esther 4:16).

A KINGDOM THAT WILL NOT FALL

Like many young professionals, I began my career focused on the millions of dollars I intended to make, the titles I would earn, the important things I would accomplish, and the impact all of this would have on my family. As the years passed, those ideas were replaced with more meaningful ones that were greater than my self-serving dreams.

Immediately after college, I lived in eastern Tennessee, where I was responsible for selling medical supplies and equipment to doctors' offices and surgery centers. In that role, I represented nearly two-thousand manufacturers and sold all types of medical supplies and equipment throughout the region. One day I'd be selling to a surgery center and the next I would be selling to a pediatric office. The work was both rewarding and lucrative.

Over time, I realized that my favorite part of the job was the people. I met some of the most incredible folks with the biggest hearts caring for patients of all ages. I also worked with an incredible vendor community, and one of my favorite reps was a gentleman named Mike.

While I was still early in my career, Mike had been in medical sales for several decades. He was selling spirometers when we first met, and we would often visit pediatric offices together to demonstrate his product. I remember how he loved people like I did, and how he would coach the nurses through a demonstration. To run the test, they would have to blow through a hollow tube as the connected device would capture various data points.

On one occasion, Mike took this demo perfor-mance to the extreme when he blew into the tube until he passed out. His ego was bruised and his head was bleeding from hitting it on a table. Thankfully, he was in a great place to receive medical care, and the doctor sutured him up right there in the clinic. He often laughed while telling that story, and as bad as it could have been, Mike took it all in stride.

Mike was a gifted salesman, and working with him was an amazing education for me. As much as I enjoyed visiting customers and selling with him, what I most appreciated was that when we were together he saw a young man full of hope and promise who was still in need of guidance. He took an active interest in my life, and I still carry the lessons I learned from him. During our first year of marriage, Mike would take Jamye and me out to dinner anytime he came within fifty miles of Johnson City.

Knowing and being known by the people with whom you work is an important part of any job. Intentional relationships create trust, linking you and your coworkers arm in arm as you set out to accomplish your joint goals. As Mike got to know Jamye and me over the years, he made it a point to share about his life with us, both the good moments and the moments that were not so good. One specific conversation I had with Mike about work and life has always stuck with me.

He had been married and divorced twice and had two grown children. The greatest advice he ever gave me was to never forget that my family was always a higher priority than my occupation. When you're a twenty-three-year-old newlywed taking on the responsibility of being a spouse, renting your first place, and working your first job, that's a difficult statement to grasp. I wanted to make as much money as possible, win all the awards, and rise through the ranks of my organization.

In a few short years, I became a father and I began to understand what Mike had been telling me. He didn't want the allure of the business, the money, and the promotion to derail my personal life and the lives of those I love.

Mike was warning me that whatever kingdom I chose to build, I needed to make sure it would not easily fall. It was the single greatest lesson I learned from Mike, and I will never forget his words. Now later in my career with a wife and two sons, those words mean more to me than any amount of money, award, or promotion. While Mike was in the second half of his career as mine was just starting, he cared enough to help me not make the same mistakes he had made.

I first met Mike more than seventeen years ago.

Since then, I have worked with hundreds of organizations that employ hundreds of thousands of individuals. I would venture to say I have engaged in over ten thousand conversations with clients, and have closed $100 million in sales across multiple industries. I have been cussed out, praised, questioned, and rewarded for my efforts. I have stood on the stages reserved for the big awards, and I have sat in the corner beaten and defeated, waiting for the bell to ring to start the next round.

Mike passed away not too long ago, and though I had not seen him in a long time, those early years partnering with him in business had a significant impact on my life.

WE ARE ROYALTY

"For such a time as this."

We have to understand that when Mordecai said these words centuries ago, people's lives were hanging in the balance, and that is still true today. Esther was faced with a choice to live a life of royalty and remain silent, or risk it all to save the lives of those who needed her to intercede on their behalf.

There are men and women around the globe

dying daily with no vision of eternity. Equal numbers of people die daily while believing that their lives have had no value, purpose, or meaning.

For some, their morning alarm sounds and they begrudgingly rise from their beds to prepare for the day ahead. They shuttle children to school, stop at Starbucks for a daily caffeine fix that stretches the limits of their budget, and find themselves working a job the rest of the day they would leave in a heartbeat if they could afford to do so. They return home exhausted from the eight-hour grind, cook dinner, sit on the couch, maybe attempt to have some kind of family time, prepare for bed, and dread the next day's alarm.

For others, the alarm sounds and their day is aimed at obtaining the "more" of life. More money, more things, more fame; more, more, more. Are they so different from the rest? Though they may appear to be happier and fully alive on the surface, these people may still be dying inside as they search in vain for value, purpose, and meaning.

There are countless men, women, and children sitting in church pews around the world who believe Kingdom building is reserved solely for pastors, ministers, and missionaries. While I am thankful for the men and women who do have those specific ministerial callings on their lives, no one who follows Jesus, regardless of vocation, is exempt from being on mission, evangelizing, and contributing to the building of the Kingdom of God. Hear me clearly; I think those callings on a man or woman's life are incredible and I am thankful for them. However, not carrying one of those titles does not excuse us from being on mission, evangelizing, and ultimately contributing to the building of God's Kingdom.

As Christians, we are called to live a life that glorifies God: that includes our business and work environments. This world has convinced us to separate our faith from our work based on the lie that tells us our identity is wrapped up in what we produce and not to whom we belong.

I know too many men and women who have built kingdoms with possessions and achievements that will not follow them into eternity. I have seen their marriages crumble, their families collapse, their finances vanish, and addictions take hold as they fall into the trap of believing that their lives and work have no meaning or purpose.

We have all heard someone say, "you can't take it with you," and have laughed because we know they are right. We can't take *it* with us, yet *it* drives us to build and build our own kingdoms, believing that if our personal kingdom is big enough, strong enough, beautiful enough, wealthy enough, and famous enough, then maybe we have shown ourselves to have great value and purpose compared to others who could not build what we have built.

Stop it! The kingdom you build is sitting on a foundation of sand and will not weather the storms of this life. It cannot stand the test of time, and no matter how impressive it is, it will ultimately fall if it is built relying on things of this world.

Why do we build upon the sand instead of building upon the rock? The headlines we see across the news and social media outlets draw our attention to issues across the world that would have us believe they are earthly concerns, but I urge you to look closer and recognize heavenly battles are being fought all around us. There is another kingdom that needs your attention. Don't fill your heart and life with treasures that fade and will prevent you from working to promote and protect the Kingdom of God.

THE SHEPHERD BOY KING

One of my favorite figures in the Bible is David, the shepherd boy who became king. We first meet David as God sends Samuel to Bethlehem, to the house of Jesse, to anoint the next king of Israel. Samuel knows God has chosen one of Jesse's sons, but he does not know which one.

Jesse calls seven of his eight sons into the presence of Samuel. Although he initially believes one of them to be the chosen king, God tells Samuel, "do not consider his appearance or his height, for I have rejected him. The Lord does not look at the things people look at. People look at the outward appearance, but the Lord looks at the heart" (1 Samuel 16:7).

Samuel asks Jesse if these are all of his sons, to which Jesse explains the youngest is out looking after the sheep. The young boy is summoned and brought before Samuel. The Lord says, "Arise and anoint him; this is the one" (1 Samuel 16:12), so Samuel takes a horn of oil and anoints David in the presence of his father and brothers. Like He did with Esther, God intervenes in the life of David, a young shepherd boy who appears to be of no stature or importance.

From that moment forward, David's life

unfolds into one of the most spectacular stories in the Bible. Entire books have been written about both his successes and failures. It is written that David was a man after God's own heart, and his life is an account of a boy turned king who understood what it meant to protect, advance, and bear witness to the King and His kingdom.

DAVID AND GOLIATH

In 1 Samuel 17, the Israelites and Philistines prepare for battle along opposite sides of the Elah Valley. Emerging from the Philistine camp, a soldier named Goliath comes forth, taunting the Israelites. He asks for a lone combatant to battle him, which would end the war and determine the victor. Goliath is a giant of a man, standing over nine feet tall and wearing more than 100 pounds of armor. His intimidation factor is obvious and no one wants to fight him. His taunting continues for forty days with no response from the Israelite army.

During these forty days, Jesse sends David to Israel's front line to take food to three of his brothers who have enlisted in Saul's army. Early one morning, David hears Goliath's insults and witnesses the Israelites retreating in fear. Something must have stirred in David's heart because he did not take kindly to the insults of Goliath. "Who is this uncircumcised Philistine that he should defy the armies of the living God?" (1 Samuel 17:26).

When David is called to speak with King Saul, he announces that he will fight Goliath. Saul takes a look at David's stature and suggests that is not an option as he is still young and not a soldier. David counters much like you would expect from any young man with a warrior's heart. He tells Saul that as a shepherd he had defended his flock from lions and bears, both of which he killed. When predators came for his sheep, David fought for their lives. As Goliath attacks his kinsmen, David is determined to fight for their lives as well, as he is sure God will protect him.

Saul relents and David rushes into the valley to fight the Philistine. Goliath hurls insults at David, "I'll give your flesh to the birds and the wild animals" (1 Samuel 17:44), but David is unphased. "This day the LORD will deliver you into my hands, and I'll strike you down and cut off your head" (1 Samuel 17:46). With a sling and a stone, David does the unimaginable and kills the giant with a single blow to Goliath's forehead. A young shepherd boy defeats the greatest soldier in the

Philistine Army, and as he promised, removes Goliath's head from his shoulders.

God spent years preparing David "for such a time as this," and in that preparation, David's confidence and conviction were born. This story is not about the strength of a shepherd boy, but the strength of God in him to stand against all odds, believing the Lord is bigger than any giant he could ever face. David was placed into circumstances where his fortitude and obedience would impact the lives of a nation, and like Esther, he acted in great faith. May we all be so bold.

Reflection

WHEN WE PAUSE TO REFLECT ON THE
course of events that have led us to this very
moment, we can see God's fingerprints over our
past. We have all faced our share of Goliaths, have
stood in uncertainty before those who have
authority over us, and have been given royal
permission to live as kingdom builders.

What situation are you in right now where you
can see God's preparation in your life "for such a
time as this?" Do not read the stories of Esther and
David believing that your life carries less purpose
or value. Just as lives were hanging in the balance as
they took their stand, lives remain at stake even
today, and you have the opportunity to intervene
and fight to protect them.

Jesus said, "The thief comes only to steal and
kill and destroy. I came that they may have life and
have it abundantly," (John 10:10). As Christians,
we know how the story ends. The incredible thing
is our individual stories are still being written, and
we still have time to be kingdom builders. Set
against the backdrop of time, our lives will last for
only a moment, but what we choose to do in that
time will have an eternal effect.

"After this I looked, and behold, a great multitude that no one could number, from every nation, from all tribes and peoples and languages, standing before the throne and before the Lamb, clothed in white robes, with palm branches in their hands . . ."

CHAPTER 3

YOUR STORY WITHIN THE STORY

A MOMENT FOR ETERNITY

The way we are living, timorous or bold, will have been our life.

— SEAMUS HEANEY

At the time of this writing, it is the Christmas season. Like many families, we have our favorite traditions, one of which is watching our favorite holiday films in the weeks leading up to Christmas day. Each year, we make a list of movies to watch with our sons, and we pull them up on one of the multiple streaming services in our home, bypassing all trailers and commercials. As much as I love the convenience of getting straight into the movie, I do miss the days of being forced to watch a good trailer that puts me on the edge of my seat.

Just as the technology for film has improved, so have the movie trailers in a $200 billion industry. Movies now often have more than one trailer, and we can view them anytime on YouTube or other streaming platforms. We no longer have to rewind a VHS tape or go to the theater to get that edge-of-your-seat feeling.

When I read the opening words of the Bible in Genesis, I imagine the greatest movie trailer of all time. The screen goes black, then there is a dramatic rise in color as a booming voice announces, "in the beginning, God created the Heavens and the Earth!" It is a short phrase, but its intensity sets the stage for the most incredible story ever told. I imagine pictures of the solar system and the Earth, with God hovering above the waters as a flash of light, traveling at a high rate of speed.

Fast-forward to the book of Revelation, and we see another incredible scene as the whole story of the Bible draws to a close. People from across the world are gathered together, representing every nation, tribe, and language as they stand before God, who is surrounded by angels, rejoicing in His presence. An orchestra plays in the background and the camera captures the momentous occasion in a full 360-degree spin around the crowd with God on the throne. There is a final dramatic beating of a drum as the screen dims again, the credits roll, and the movie is over–or is it?

Genesis and Revelation tell us so much about the beginning and the end, but what about the pages in between? What about the countless stories throughout history that bridge these two epic periods of time? What about your story? Where does it fit in this larger narrative? While our lives last but a moment in time, they hold eternal value. If we look closely, we will find that the story of "us" is a story within His story—the greatest story ever told.

IN THE BEGINNING

Within the opening words of the Bible, you are immediately faced with a choice that will determine how you view everything else that follows. In the first verse, in just ten words, the Bible declares God to be the divine creator who set time into motion. There is an immediate choice in regard to belief. These first words demand a response; do you believe God created the heavens and earth? Do you believe He has always existed? Do you recognize and accept this event to be the beginning of all things created in this universe? How we respond to this first verse sets the stage for how we will respond to God in other areas of our lives.

For some, the idea that God has always existed and created the universe out of nothing is unfathomable and inexplicable. Start asking around and you will receive a number of responses rooted in science or something else beyond the simple belief that God is capable of doing more than we can imagine.

Others will read these words and question them with an underlying desire to learn more. They may believe in God but struggle to understand how He could create the universe. They may not be fully bought into the idea, but curiosity can breed more questions and further examination.

Then there are those that fully accept God to be God. He is the Alpha and Omega, the creator of heaven and earth, and nothing was created until God spoke it into existence.

To be clear, I understand there are people who struggle with or question God's existence and the words written about Him in scripture. Working out your own salvation and beliefs is a process. At the same time, when I flip a light switch in my home, the lights either turn on or off. There is a degree of choosing to believe that leaves no room for unbelief. Doubt and uncertainty are very different from disbelief, so please do not think you must possess all knowledge of God and the Bible to believe in Him. However, do not think you can call yourself a Christian and remain in disbelief of God's word.

CREATED TO CREATE

Jamye and I agree that if we do nothing else in our lifetimes, we need to make sure our children know the Lord and grow in relationship with Him. There are times I fail miserably, but I am grateful my wife fails far less often than I do when exemplifying Jesus to our sons. She has an education background and taught preschool and elementary school students early in our marriage, so she has a true gift for teaching children that I do not possess. Still, every now and again there are lessons in our house that need to come from dad.

A few years ago, Clark and I needed to have *the talk*. You know the one I'm talking about, and as you're reading these words you're likely experiencing flashbacks to the talks you have given or received, and you're either smiling or cringing. Personally, I had mixed emotions about this talk with my son and was not sure how to deliver it in an effective way. I have friends who have given their kids books to read and told them to come back with questions. One friend shared with me that *the talk* with his son was going great until his wife walked in, at which point the son became so embarrassed about what he had just learned that he ran out of the room.

I never want to forget every moment of that day I spent with Clark having *the talk*. We went deer hunting early in the morning and had a huge breakfast with biscuits the size of my head. We talked about the generations of men who came before us in our lineage, and drove past the houses my grandparents and great-grandparents once owned.

It was a special day. I want my sons to step into manhood by claiming the inheritance we discussed earlier. I want them to know they were created by a creator who wants to give them the opportunity to bring forth life. I want them to believe that God created all of us to bring Himself glory, and that they have an opportunity to participate in the story that started in Genesis 1:1.

CREATED TO SERVE

One of the most eye-opening experiences of my life came from praying with and feeding the homeless. For just over a year, each Friday morning, I would meet with several friends to walk the streets of our city handing out biscuits, bottles of water, and socks as we prayed with the homeless. We were not very organized, but we saw a need and wanted to do something about it.

The first morning we were armed with fifty sausage biscuits and a few cases of bottled water. We didn't know where we were going, and I was a bit anxious about the whole ordeal. We had only driven a couple blocks when we saw a lady sitting in her wheelchair outside the doors of a large church. We parked our cars, and I took the lead as we approached her.

What happened next blew me away. As soon as she realized we were going to stop and speak with her, the woman pulled a comb from her pocket and began to run it through her unkempt hair. My heart broke. I had spent the previous night in a comfortable bed beside my wife, in a home with locked doors and a controlled climate, and had eaten a warm dinner. This woman looked at me with a mix of apprehension and hope in her eyes, and all I could do was say, "you don't need to comb your hair, you look beautiful."

She smiled in a way that said "thank you" as she put the comb back into her pocket. I handed her food and a bottle of water, and we began a conversation like any two strangers would. Her name was Mary, and we learned she had been on the streets for a long time. I was relieved she was receptive to our offering, but I didn't want to pry too much into her life as we were hoping to build rapport over the next several months.

A number of weeks went by, and we got to know Mary a little bit better with each visit. One Friday morning we went to see her, but she was nowhere to be found. Another homeless individual told us Mary was very sick and had been placed in the hospital and would lose her foot. One of the guys in our small Friday morning group was a doctor with ties to the hospital. He was able to find out where she was, so our team went to see and pray with her. It was one of the last times we saw Mary, and although I found out a little about her life and her Kentucky roots, I regret that I never learned her full story.

I learned a lot from Mary, and there were many others we encountered that year. I hope to never forget the people of all different ethnicities, socioeconomic backgrounds, genders, and ages. If you don't think there is power in someone's story, I encourage you to get out of your comfort zone and start a conversation with a homeless person in your town. You might surprise yourself with what you can learn from them and, if appropriate, how you might be able to help them in their journey.

CAREER OF SERVICE

In 2022, we celebrated my father-in-law's retirement. I have known Eddie since I was a senior in high school, so I've had more than twenty years to learn from him and his work. I have witnessed how he cares for his clients and goes above and beyond to make sure they are set up for success. On the night of his retirement celebration, I saw emotion pour out of him and others who shared about his character and his career that was marked by humble service to the community. It was a wonderful night to honor and celebrate a man who hates to be celebrated.

Eddie joined the Marine Corps immediately following high school. His boot camp stories are hysterical. My sons and I even had the opportunity to visit Parris Island with him as he shared some of those stories—a memory I will never forget. After the Marine Corps, he moved into several other positions here in South Carolina before spending the last twenty years selling surveying equipment across the state. Having been in sales for most of my career, I have always enjoyed sharing stories of success and failure from our work. It has been great to know that some of the situations I have faced are not unique to me and that even a guy who is as sharp and tenured as Eddie has faced obstacles and challenges.

It was an incredible night. There was a sense of wonder and beauty in the fact that Eddie was celebrating retirement while there were two young children in the house and a number of us in stages of life that fell between those two extremes.

On the heels of Eddie's retirement party, I thought about the concept of time and how quickly it goes by. Two-thousand years before Eddie's party, Jesus came to be the savior of a people who could not save themselves, and somehow, those very same people are allowed to participate in the greatest story ever told.

The Importance of a Dash

A great friend once shared the importance of the little dash each of us will have in the brief span of our time on Earth. When we are born and when we die, our life is recorded in a summary of dates with a little dash between them. It feels ludicrous to imagine that a life could be summed up in such a short method, but there is incredible power in that little dash.

Everywhere we turn, there is someone telling us how to live our dash. We are bombarded with advertisements and opinions about how we should look, what kind of car to drive, where to vacation, how to spend our money, and how to maximize our lives. I don't have a problem with someone trying to sell me their products, and I don't have any issue with others sharing their opinions when it leads to greater conversations. However, I do take issue with the idea that our lives are to be lived in a manner that solely focuses on our needs, wants, and desires.

The older I get, the more I think about my dash. I think about all the things I have cared about and how much of my time and attention they have received over the years. I look at my wife and sons and think about how quickly time moves and how I can't get it back. I have moments where I ask myself if I have been the husband and father they've needed. They will tell you I have been present and have worked hard to provide a life for them, but I know I can do more.

When I look back and ponder the past, it gives me fuel to make the future greater for them. As I turn forty years old around the time of this writing, building a greater future for my children looks different than it did ten years ago. A decade ago, my success criteria revolved more around securing our future. It was about making a certain amount of money, investing and saving, and knowing we could live a life of comfort. It was about giving my family their wildest dreams, building generational wealth, and leaving a legacy.

The human side of me, as a husband and father, wants to give my family everything this world can offer. I want to take them on memorable trips, I hope to leave money for generations of children I will never meet, and I want to see my sons live their wildest dreams as they grow into young men. Still, something has changed inside of me. I don't want my dash to be about *me* any longer, and I don't want to live in a manner that makes my children think their dash is all about them.

So many people speak about leaving a legacy. We see names on buildings, awards, and honors being bestowed upon others, and we realize we want to be important and remembered for doing something amazing with our lives. Again, it's not a bad thing to impact the lives of others and be honored with those accolades if they happen, but living to prove you were someone deserving of those honors is an exhausting life. Legacy is not about what you accomplished—legacy is about living a life that points others to Christ.

As parents and leaders in our homes, we want to give our children everything we can. We want them to chase their dreams, see the world, and to live a big life so their dash tells an incredible story. We must show them an example of what it means to live a life reflective of a dash well lived.

Too often, we make this life about *us* and pursue things that fill *us* with temporary joy and treasures. The single most important thing we can do as parents is to help our children know Jesus and grow in Him. That is how we give our children everything, how they live the fullest of lives, and how we make that "dash" between our birth and death date really count. As Linda Ellis eloquently states in *The Dash Poem:*

> *So, when your eulogy is being read*
> *With your life's actions to rehash . . .*
> *Would you be proud of the things they say*
> *About how you spent YOUR dash?*

As human beings, we have the opportunity to not only live incredible stories but to become incredible storytellers. It's a natural component of how we communicate. We tell stories about a child's first steps, their first home run, meeting the girl in math class, the nerve-racking job interview, the first home purchase, the triumphs and struggles of our jobs, and even what happened on our way to the grocery store this week.

We constantly create and tell stories, and yet I find it fascinating we are living in the middle of the greatest story ever told. For every beginning, we know there must be an end. Our lives start with a birth story and end with stories being told about how we lived our dash.

Reflection

UNLIKE MOST STORIES IN OUR LIVES, WE know how the story of God's love for His creation ends, and it's spectacular. I'll challenge you as I challenge myself moving forward - if God created the Heavens and the Earth, and He created us to live a life that points others to Him, will we give Him everything, including our work? Will we entrust Him with our finances, our parenting, our futures, our dreams, and our identities, in addition to eternity?

As natural-born storytellers, what story will we share no matter the audience or venue? Will it be the story of Jesus, or will it be the story of our own lives? Will our dash point to God? Will it express thankfulness for His reign and authority over our lives? Did we love those entrusted to our care? Did we acknowledge the homeless and give a voice to the voiceless? Did we live, or simply survive?

We are living in the age between Jesus' resurrection and His imminent return. We are living in the New Testament and will one day leave this world to spend an eternity either with Jesus or apart from Him. As believers, it is imperative we do not hold the story of Jesus, the story of God's redeeming love for His creation, to ourselves. We are all called to share the gospel and reach those who have yet to hear His name.

"Go therefore and make
disciples of all nations,
baptizing them in the
name of the Father and of
the Son and of the Holy
Spirit . . ."

CHAPTER 4

A COLLECTIVE CALLING

THE MISSION OF EVERY CHRISTIAN

Satan has another strategy to oppose the
advancement of God's kingdom and the fulfill-
ment of God's mission to be glorified among the
nations. This may be the most effective among
all his tactics: convincing Christians that
missions is optional.

— JERRY RANKIN

"How long have you known about this
man Jesus, and why did it take you so
long to come here and tell us about
Him?" These words were spoken by a ninety-year-
old woman in a small hut from a village on the

other side of the world in the 21st century. A missionary had come to her small community, and the older woman listened intently as the missionary spoke with the local chieftain. As she was explaining Jesus to the chief, trying to gain his permission to visit the people and share the gospel with them, this woman heard of Jesus for the first time in her nearly century-long life.

This story shakes me to the core. I can't imagine speaking with someone who's never heard the name of Jesus. Everywhere we turn, technology and information flow freely from our phones, computers, and televisions, sharing all kinds of information about the various religions of the world. How can someone in the 21st century not know the name of Jesus? As shocking as it sounds, it's not as uncommon as you may expect.

Search for the statistics through any given missions agency, and you will find there are *many* ears that have yet to hear the Good News. There are an estimated total of at least three billion unreached people in the world, which is roughly forty percent of Earth's population. Being *unreached* means having little to no access to the gospel of Jesus Christ. Three billion unreached people is an alarming number, as well as a statistic many churchgoers may not know.

I have always been fascinated with missions and the lives of missionaries. I thought (and even hoped) for years that God would call me to international missions in Africa. I'm aware that many areas of Africa are thriving spiritually, but I also know there are many communities lacking access to the gospel, and there is no place on Earth so full of believers that there are no people in need of Jesus. So, why Africa? I don't have a concrete answer as to why it's been on my heart, but I've always felt like God has something for me to do there.

While God may still choose to move our family to Africa, my mission field has looked very different from what I anticipated. In fact, it is so different that I didn't even know it was a mission field for the longest time. Because we often associate missions work exclusively with international missionaries sent to the far ends of the earth, we rarely discuss the missions fields in our work and local communities.

Jesus spoke the words of Mathew 28:19 to His disciples soon after He was raised from the grave, just before He ascended into Heaven. I have read these words over and over, and for the longest time thought they were only for missionaries. How could I be on mission with Jesus while working in a business that was not associated with the church? It didn't make sense for years, until I finally began to meet and speak with traditional missionaries about their calling and how they view missions.

The closest I have come to international missions is interacting with these folks who have lived across the world serving in that capacity. Their stories leave me feeling equally fascinated and convicted. What they've shown me is a shift in missions and evangelism happening around the world. The American church is filled with folks struggling to see their life's work as a mission, which we are all called to whether or not that calling leads us to the international mission field.

I don't want you to wait any longer to bridge the gap between faith and work. I hope the following missionary stories provide reassurance that your work is very important to God.

These folks have taught me a lot about what it means to view my work as a mission field. Their names have been changed for security purposes, but I haven't edited their stories or the experiences I've had with each of them.

We are all called to be on mission with God— to declare His word to all the world, but that doesn't mean each of us is called to do it in the same manner. Columbia International University is just a few miles from my home, and its motto is "To Know Him and to Make Him Known." First, know God, and then share Him with those you meet. That is the essence of being on mission, and while some will go to foreign lands, others will have opportunities to share Jesus in their workplace without leaving town. Both are important and divine in nature when they are ordained by God.

MORGAN

I first met Morgan when she came to speak at a church-hosted missions event many years ago. Her passion was marketplace missions, which is the exact idea I am promoting here. She was the first person to show me that our ideas of missionary work need to evolve and that our vocations may be leading us to the greatest mission field we will encounter in this lifetime.

Morgan has worked as a marketplace missionary across the globe. She specifically has a heart for people living in what is often called the "10/40 window"–a region of the world home to roughly four-billion people who represent sixty-eight countries "located from 10 degrees south to 40 degrees north of the equator." Statistics for this part of the world are unthinkable, and I have included some of them below so you can further understand why this region is so important to those in full-time missions work.

From Win1040.org:

- *Two-thirds of the world's population — 4 billion people — live in the 10/40 Window.*
- *95% of these 4 billion people are unevangelized.*
- *87% are the poorest of the poor, living on an average of only $250 per family annually.*
- *In many of the 69 nations, witnessing the Christian gospel is illegal and will result in imprisonment or death.*
- *45 of the 50 worst countries in the world for persecution of Christians are in the 10/40 Window.*
- *Child prostitution and child slavery run rampant in many of these nations.*
- *Horrific abuse of women and children remains unchecked, including an epidemic of pedophilia.*

- *A majority of the world's terrorist organizations are based in the 10/40 Window, and children as young as 18 months old are trained to be Jihad soldiers.*

Though the needs are both desperate and urgent, only 5¢ out of every $100 spent on missions globally is directed toward the 10/40 Window. That's 0.0005% of all mission money designated to bring the gospel to 66% of the world's population!

As persecution is intensifying against 21st-century Christians, the ability to freely travel while sharing the gospel is becoming increasingly difficult and dangerous. As you can see in the statistics above, many circumstances make the process of reaching the world incredibly dangerous. Regardless of how difficult it may be, we cannot let ourselves be deterred. As the world tightens its grip on where missionaries can work freely, there is an idea that equipping missionaries for the workplace may open new doors where others are quickly closing.

If a missionary is able to work within a community, they are able to rely less on church-based funding and will spend considerably more time with people during the work week. Think about how much time we spend working and how much we get to know about our coworkers. Some of my best friends and mentors have come through the businesses in which I have spent years working alongside them with similar interests and goals. Why would we think this model couldn't be successful for international missions?

Morgan has taught me so much about marketplace missions, discipleship, and what it means to *live as one who is sent*. Her career has been focused on the global missions field, and I have never met anyone quite like her. Her desire to see people have a relationship with God is evident as soon as you meet her. She and her family are an incredible example of surrendering their lives to follow their calling, and I am grateful for the many conversations we've had and her investing in my life as I wrestle with God's calling on my life through my work.

DONNA

Like Morgan, I met Donna at a missions event hosted by my church. I am glad to have met them several years apart because I was able to relate more to Donna's story as a result of having learned from Morgan and her discipleship in my life.

Donna has worked in the global mission field for roughly twenty years since the early 2000s. She has traveled to over seventy countries and recently returned from Ukraine just before war broke out with Russia in 2022. The story I shared about the ninety-year-old woman at the beginning of this chapter came from Donna. She was the missionary sitting in that hut, and she has *many* more stories just like that one.

Donna has had to fight off kidnappers, hang on to the outside of a moving train, escape from being stoned, and has bathed with piranhas in the Amazon River. As she shared these stories, I kept thinking about the "difficult things" I have been through in my career, and they paled in comparison to the life-or-death nature of hers. We ought not to compare our lives to others' lives to the point of feeling superior or inferior, but comparison does have value when assessing if we are doing all we are capable of doing to share the gospel. That's the question I've been asking myself since meeting Donna–am I doing everything I can to spread the gospel?

Donna recently shared another story that has stuck with me. She and her translator were approaching a village when a man in the distance began to run towards them, shouting loudly as he approached. As he came closer, the translator told her he was shouting, "Are you the ones I have been waiting for?!" It gave me chills when Donna first shared that line. Once the man reached them, he asked the same question again, then explained that someone had once shared with him the name of Jesus, but he's waited years for someone to come and tell him more. Just like the woman in the hut, this man lived in a place with no access to the gospel, waiting for someone to arrive and share the good news of Jesus as a missionary.

I told Donna about meeting and learning from Morgan and asked her opinion on marketplace missions. Like Morgan, Donna believes the marketplace and our businesses serve as an opportunity to develop new strategies for global missions. In fact, one of the ways her team is approaching global evangelization is to work with international workers who are living away from their homelands but hope to eventually return. If these people are currently living and working in a place where they can be reached and equipped, they may present the greatest opportunity to take Jesus back to their home countries.

STEVE

Steve's path to becoming an international missionary involved many twists and turns, but ultimately led him from his business to the international mission field with his wife and family. For him to leave a steady job, guaranteed income, and the safety of his community—uprooting his family and leaving the country to share God with others—is nothing short of amazing.

When I think about Steve's journey to the mission field, there are three specific moments that stand out.

First, I hosted a vision casting event years ago and asked him to attend and speak with the group about what he was doing in South America. Morgan was there as well, and it was special to see them together speaking from experiences they had shared. Their mutual love of missions led them to work with people groups on two different continents, yet their emotions and their stories shared so many parallels.

As he was speaking, Steve became visibly emotional. He spoke of the lostness he encountered in his work while he struggled to hold back the tears. As he spoke, I saw a similar emotional response from Morgan. The pain Steve felt for the lost as he spoke was a level of compassion I and every person who calls themselves a Christian should have for the lost.

A second thing that stands out is how Steve expresses his heart's desire for missions to both God *and* his wife. When God calls a husband or wife into service, He calls their spouse and entire family. I had a chance to hear directly from Steve's wife about the process of choosing to go into full-time mission work. She admitted her uncertainty and lack of desire to pick up and move, but over time God worked in her heart and she and Steve became aligned in His vision for their lives. Steve prayed for confirmation from God and a stirring in his wife's heart, and God answered both prayers.

Finally, it has impressed me how Steve has managed to not only be obedient in his calling but how he's done it in a way that involves his entire family. He has set an example for his children of how to discern and live out God's calling, and to do it fully surrendered. By example, he has prepared his children to hear God's voice and to surrender their lives.

So many things can keep us frozen in fear and not moving into God's calling. We question if we truly hear His voice, or if it's our own thoughts and ideas fantasizing about what we should do. Is now the right time? Am I capable of doing the work? What about my job, my home, my family, my plan? How will I survive financially, and what if I can't learn another language? What if I go and find out that I made a mistake?

HAILEY

I have never actually met Hailey but I have known her father, Jack, for several years through my work. While at a networking event, Jack asked how the writing process was going for my book. I shared some details of the outline and message I hope to bring to my readers. He affirmed several items I intended to share in this book, and let me know that his daughter was preparing for a short-term mission trip.

Jack's daughter is a recent college graduate who feels God leading her to the other side of the world. While I don't know Hailey, I know the kind of man her father is and how hard he's worked to financially provide for his family while pointing them to Christ. He may not be accompanying her on this trip, but he has led his family in such a way that she knows how to hear God speaking in her life and trusts Him with her future.

I don't know what lies ahead for Hailey, but I am excited to watch her journey unfold and am grateful for the work her father does, along with his example to his family, that has allowed her to consider this next step in her life.

Sharing the stories of these individuals—Morgan, Donna, Steve, and Hailey—reminds me of when I took a few seminary classes years ago and had an opportunity to hear from someone working with students interested in missionary work. When asked what the number one reason is why students who plan to be missionaries don't follow through on those plans, can you guess what she answered? It's *money*, which isn't a shock. She explained that most students accumulate so much debt through school loans and cost of living expenses while in college that they delay their plans in order to pay off their debts. As a result, either the excitement and fire for mission work will fade or the debt is replaced by the desire to earn more, and they never make it to the mission field.

It's a sad reality, and as much as I hate money being a constraint, I can also understand how it may become an obstacle. Hailey continues to raise financial support, and it's a special opportunity to witness someone recently out of school fully trusting God.

THE GREAT COMMISSION

Jesus' words at the end of Mathew's gospel are often referred to as *The Great Commission*.

Then Jesus came to them and said, "All authority in heaven and on earth has been given to me. Therefore go and make disciples of all nations, baptizing them in the name of the Father and of the Son and of the Holy Spirit, and teaching them to obey everything I have commanded you. And surely I am with you always, to the very end of the age" (Matthew 28:18-20).

Jesus left His heavenly throne to enter a fallen world and live under the authority of God while redeeming mankind. With His time on earth complete, Jesus gave a final command to His disciples as they prepared for what lay ahead. Many people read this passage and think His command is found in the word "go," but it's not. The original text translates "as you are going" or "while you are going."

Read this verse again replacing "therefore" with "while you are going," and you will understand that the command follows. The fullness of the command is found in the act of making disciples of all nations, baptizing them, and teaching them all they had learned. Jesus didn't leave the disciples to do this alone either; He gave them the Holy Spirit as a helper who would always be present as they went out into the world.

As Jesus ascends into Heaven, the disciples' next chapter begins. Their stories have been recorded and preserved for centuries. In their efforts to live out Jesus' command, they too were often beaten, mocked, tried, and killed–several by crucifixion.

Jesus' command doesn't end with the original disciples. His authority remains, and the command to *make disciples of all nations* carries into our lives even now. We are called to live out the *Great Commission*, and though the specifics may look different for each of us, this is the collective calling of every Christian.

Some of us will be called to foreign lands, to live with people who have never heard the name of Jesus. Others of us will be called to support those missionaries with our finances and prayers. For those of us not called to the international field, we should consider how God has us on mission right where we are living.

I want us to walk boldly in faith, whether it's

through Africa or just a few miles away from our homes. Living out the *Great Commission* comes with a cost for each of us. For the disciples, it cost them security, financial gain, friendships, their homes, and for most of them, their lives. I don't know what it will cost you and me, but I hope we are willing, and dare I say eager, to find out.

Reflection

IT IS ASTOUNDING HOW MANY PEOPLE living in the 21st century have little to no access to the gospel. How can it be that men, women, and children living in modern times have not heard the name of Jesus? Does it break our hearts? Does it move us to action, or do we dismiss these people, expecting our missionaries to reach them instead of becoming involved ourselves?

The somber reality is that billions of people living without the gospel will result in billions of people facing an eternity outside of Heaven. Some people will water down the truth and say that God wouldn't allow that to happen, or you can be a good person and still find your way into His presence for eternity, because that sounds nice and inclusive. They want to only believe in a God who has no wrath or judgment, but that's not our God.

The Bible tells us in Philippians 2 that every knee will bow, and every tongue confess that Jesus Christ is Lord. He endured the cross for our benefit, and has given us the greatest gift in salvation that we could not earn or afford. With that gift, we have been given a responsibility and the authority to share with others what He has done for us. Your mission field may not be overseas, but that doesn't mean you can't be involved with international missions through various avenues of support. Some of us are called to live globally, and others are called to mission fields within their homes, communities, businesses, and vocations.

"... And Jesus said to
Simon, 'Do not be afraid;
from now on you will be
catching men.'"

CHAPTER 5

THE GREAT COMMISSION

YOUR INDIVIDUAL CALLING

The one supreme business of life is to find God's
plan for your life and live it.

— E. STANLEY JONES

Christmas is my favorite time of year,
closely followed by Easter. I love the
warmth of spring rising over the
winter's chill. At Christmas we celebrate the birth
of our Savior, and at Easter His conquering of
death. He left an empty tomb and canceled our
unpayable debt to sin. Easter brings the beloved
Easter egg hunts with our children, pastel
matching outfits, choir presentations, and large

family gatherings around kitchen tables. I love the Easter traditions and the smiles across the faces of children running through the yard with baskets full of eggs.

Before Jesus rose from the grave, He was first betrayed by Judas, beaten and scourged, brought before the Pharisees and Pilate in a bogus trial, publicly mocked, and crucified.

The gospels give us incredible insight into these events that occurred in the hours leading up to Jesus' crucifixion. Matthew's account tells us that Jesus was crucified with two criminals, one on His left and the other on His right. However, only Luke's account gives us the details of the verbal exchange between Jesus and these criminals as they hung from their crosses.

Here is the scene: Jesus hangs on the cross with nails driven through His hands and feet. His body is ravaged from the beating He took at the hands of the Romans. His flesh has been ripped from its frame and a crown of thorns rests upon His brow. The cross represents an evil and horrendous death and serves as a deterrent to onlookers who may be thinking of breaking the law themselves. The beating and the nails are enough to kill a man, but crucifixion brings suffering as victims struggle to breathe and become asphyxiated under their own weight. It is a bloody sight, and the Savior of the World chooses to remain and bear the weight of the cross as a propitiation for our sin.

As the hours pass, there is no doubt the criminals on either side of Jesus begin to realize who He is. They begin to panic, and through desperate and labored breath, one of the criminals shouts "Aren't you the Messiah? Save yourself and us!" (Luke 23:39). This reminds me of Satan tempting Jesus in the wilderness to abandon His earthly mission. Jesus was prepared for the mockery from this man, just like He was prepared when He was tempted by Satan in the wilderness, remaining steadfast in His mission.

Suddenly, the other criminal begins to speak, "Don't you fear God . . . since you are under the same sentence? We are punished justly, for we are getting what our deeds deserve. But this man has done nothing wrong . . . Jesus, remember me when you come into your kingdom" (Luke 23:40-42). Hearing the second criminal, Luke tells us, "Jesus answered him, 'Truly I tell you, today you will be with me in paradise'" (Luke 23:43).

In spite of the gore and horror of the crucifixion, we see a beautiful moment between Jesus and this criminal. The man didn't have time to perform good works, pay back the victims of his crimes, or be baptized and have perfect Sunday attendance. Instead, in his final moments, with very little life and breath remaining in his lungs, the man pleads with Jesus to save him not from his physical death but from his spiritual death.

It's easy to say "we all fall short," but this man's life had not just fallen short; he was out of time! As only Jesus can, He shows us that every person on this earth has a chance to be saved as long as there's breath in their body. We have an example of someone with nowhere left to turn, fixing their eyes on Jesus. We may not like it, we may not think it's fair, we may think it's phony or even a last resort to save oneself that is insincere, but when Jesus saves a man who deserved death, what we think He should do doesn't really matter.

In reality, we are all like the criminals on the cross, but which one are we? If we find ourselves to be humbled before Jesus, seeking His assurance of Heaven, what will we do to save the one who hurls insults and cares only for himself?

Each of us is given a unique opportunity to be on mission with God. He calls us out of different backgrounds and circumstances while sending us to different places. Just as we have a collective calling as the church to go forth and make disciples, so do we as individuals.

Fisher of Men

The story of the criminals on the cross forces each of us to face the reality of our own crimes against God and our need for a savior. It also reminds us that there are billions of people on this planet who are *also* in need of a savior. It is one thing to be saved, but it is another to be a witness and to share the gift you have received in Christ. We have talked about the collective calling and mission of all Christians as the body of Christ, but what does it look like on an individual level? What about those of us that are not called to be pastors, worship leaders, or missionaries, and don't work for church organizations? Did God create us only to be a part of the church while seeking our individual desires first, or is there complimentary work between the collective and the individual?

We have already seen how God used Esther to save an entire race of people; how she went from an orphaned girl to a heroic queen. Her story is only one of the many we see in the Bible where men and women are brought into their unique calling to serve and carry out the will of God. As Jesus calls the original twelve disciples to follow Him, we get a glimpse of how He can take one person's unique gifts, skills, and talents, and use them in a totally different manner for the Kingdom.

Like many of the men and women called to serve God in the Bible, Simon appears to be an ordinary man. He made a living catching fish until an encounter with Jesus on the waters of Lake Gennesaret.

If you have ever tried fishing, you know that when you cast a line into the water, there is only so much you can do to give yourself the best chance of reeling in a fish. Modern boats are equipped with fish finders. Some people like to put a bobber on their line so they see a fish strike. Baits come in every shape, color, size, and scent to attract fish. While the technology of modern fishing is very different from the fishing of Simon's time, there is one inevitable truth that remains the same—when you cast, there's no guarantee you'll catch anything. There are elements of faith and persistence that go hand-in-hand with fishing—faith that caring will produce a fish and persistence to keep trying until you do.

In Luke 5, Jesus is preaching to a crowd beside

the lake when He decides to step into Simon's boat, asking him to push out into the shallow waters. Jesus continues to teach from the boat, and when He is done tells Simon, "Put out into the deep and let down your nets for a catch" (Luke 5:4). Simon addresses Jesus as "master," and before he throws the nets into the water, explains how they had been fishing all night without catching anything. The text makes it sound as if Simon is annoyed with Jesus' request. Simon is a professional fisherman; if he didn't catch fish the previous night, wouldn't he know best about when and where to fish next?

Regardless, Simon goes through the motions of casting the nets into the water and proceeds to pull in the catch of his life! So many fish filled the nets that they began to break and he had to signal for other boats to come assist in hauling the catch to shore. When the other boats joined him, the fish became so heavy that their boats began to sink. It would have surely been an incredible sight for all who had gathered.

In verse eight, Simon falls upon his face at Jesus' knees saying "Depart from me, for I am a sinful man, O Lord." His encounter with Jesus mirrors Isaiah's encounter with God. Just like Isaiah, Simon recognizes his sin and knows he is in the presence of true holiness, rendering him unable to stand. The Seraphim touched Isaiah's unclean lips with the coal purifying them in an instant as Isaiah prepared to be placed into service as God's prophet. For Simon, Jesus instructs him not to fear saying, "from now on, you will be catching men" (Luke 5:10).

From now on you will be catching men–this phrase changes everything for Simon. The very same God who gave him his unique gifts, skills, and talents to be a professional fisherman is now going to take those same gifts, skills, and talents and leverage them in a way Simon never could have imagined. It is a monumental shift in how Simon understood his DNA as a fisherman. His profession had prepared him for his purpose in God's Kingdom. God didn't call a priest, rabbi, or political figure, He called a fisherman who made a living casting out nets in faith that they would be filled with a catch that could feed and clothe him.

Before I tell you what happens next, I want you to think about something God has placed on your heart that you know you need to do, or that you feel He is leading you towards. It could be a mission trip, a new job or ministry, or maybe even a volunteering opportunity. If God told you it was time to pursue that thing, would you obey Him and move forward without hesitation? Would you ask Him to give you more time, to hold on a little longer so you can close one more deal, save a little more money, or wait for your children to get older because you think what He's asking of you may be too dangerous?

I understand that hesitation. It is easy to say we *believe* and *trust* Him with our lives, but the moment we feel Him moving us outside our comfort zone, something changes. I find it strange that we as believers consider it an option to negotiate with God about something that requires faith when we can't see the end result. Even as I am writing, I am confronted with that hesitation. I know what it is to wrestle with uncertainty, but if we continue reading in Luke, there is a critical truth that may turn our fear into beautiful surrender as we focus on Jesus and not ourselves.

Simon and the other boats eventually find their way to dry land with the catch in tow, and the incredible calling of Simon to be a fisher of men appears to be the end of the story unless you read the next verse. "And when they had brought their boats to land, they left everything and followed him" (Luke 5:11). If you are not picking your jaw up off the floor, I need you to read that line again. This is without a doubt the biggest catch of

Simon's life, and nowhere do we read that Simon sold the fish to make sure he had money in his pocket as he followed Jesus. There was no negotiating with Jesus about what would happen next, or the timeline for when he and the others would follow Him.

No! The text says they left everything on the shore and followed Jesus! The pull of the fish, the lure of the money they could make, and the comfort they could afford could not compete with the call to follow Jesus. Simon and the others surrendered their financial security to Jesus. They surrendered their physical well-being to Jesus. They surrendered their plans, hopes, and dreams to Jesus. Simon even surrendered his identity, as Jesus would call him "Cephas," which means "rock" in Aramaic and translates to "Peter" in Greek.

THE DAMASCUS ROAD

Saul's calling was a dramatically different experience than that of Simon's. He hated anyone who followed Jesus and was a persecutor of those followers. Traveling to Damascus with murderous intent, Saul encounters Jesus in a moment that changes the course of both his life and church history.

"Now as he went on his way, he approached Damascus, and suddenly a light from heaven shone around him. And falling to the ground, he heard a voice saying to him, 'Saul, Saul, why are you persecuting me?' And he said, 'Who are you, Lord?' And he said, 'I am Jesus, whom you are persecuting'" (Acts 9:3-5).

Damascus was the capital city of Syria and reportedly had a large population of believers seeking refuge. Paul was heading there to find anyone he could that followed Jesus in order to bring them back "bound" to Jerusalem (Acts 9:2). He never expected the very God those believers followed to intercept him on his route and force him to his knees. An attack on Jesus' followers was an attack on Jesus himself, and Saul was about to answer for his actions, but not in the way you would expect.

As Saul rose to his feet, his eyes were open but he was unable to see. Blinded, his men led him into the city where he remained without sight for three days. Saul must have thought his life was ruined, but Jesus had other plans. There was a disciple in Damascus named Ananias who would have been the type of person Saul would have been after had he not been blinded.

In a vision, Jesus calls to Ananias who replies, "Here I am, Lord" (Acts 9:10). Jesus informs him there is a man from Tarsus, named Saul, who is praying and waiting on Ananias to lay hands on him and restore his sight. Saul's reputation precedes him and Ananias is unsettled, replying, "Lord, I have heard from many about this man, how much evil he has done to your saints at Jerusalem. And here he has authority from the chief priests to bind all who call on your name" (Acts 9:13-14).

Jesus tells Ananias to go as He instructed, and explains that Saul will be a "chosen instrument of mine to carry my name before the Gentiles and kings and the children of Israel" (Acts 9:15). Do not miss this! Jesus is telling Ananias that He will redeem the life of a man who hated Him in order to preach to both Jews and Gentiles, and not only those two people groups but to kings!

Ananias does as Jesus commands, and when he finds Saul, he lays his hands upon him. "Immediately something like scales fell from his eyes, and he regained his sight" (Acts 9:18). Jesus worked through Ananias to provide supernatural healing to a sinner that had not deserved it. The Bible says

Saul was also baptized, which gives us a remarkable image of redemption, mercy, and grace. Jesus himself was baptized in Mark 1:9, and to see Him bringing Saul into His fellowship and service through baptism is an incredible image of how Jesus can transform someone's life.

Saul had also been a tentmaker, and much like Simon Peter, the purpose of his trade was transferred from personal gain to financially supporting his ministry as he spread the gospel. There are no coincidences with Jesus, and it seems as if Saul was being prepared for his ministry long before he knew where God would use him.

Saul became one of the greatest figures in the early church. As his actions spread throughout the Christian community after his Damascus experience, he was often referred to by the name of Paul. It appears that his internal transformation carried over into a new physical identification that was greater than his past. Paul would live out his days serving God. His letters to the Thessalonians, Galatians, Ephesians, Philippians, Colossians, Philemon, Timothy, and Titus are all recorded in the New Testament.

Paul was quick to share about his transformation and remind others of Jesus' unfathomable grace. In the third chapter of Philippians, Paul writes, "watch out for those dogs, those evildoers, those mutilators of the flesh. For it is we who are the circumcision, we who serve God by his Spirit, who boast in Christ Jesus, and who put no confidence in the flesh—though I myself have reasons for such confidence. If someone else thinks they have reasons to put confidence in the flesh, I have more" (Philippians 3:2-4).

Reflection

GOD CALLS IMPERFECT PEOPLE INTO HIS perfect presence. People who, because of their sin, deserve wrath and condemnation rather than grace and forgiveness. Just like the criminal on the cross, each of us as sinners must come face-to-face with our ruined state so that we can witness God's mercy and redemption, both of which lead to a new life. Thank God He cares enough to pursue and transform us from sinner to saint!

Let's stop negotiating with ourselves and with God and move from where we are to where He wants to take us. As we are pulled to live the life we've designed in contrast to the life Jesus calls us to, let's remember Simon Peter's surrender to Jesus' ministry and Paul's transformation from adversary to ally. If we don't, we may become like a man who couldn't part with his earthly wealth to gain Heaven's treasure.

As the body of Christ, we have both a collective and individual calling on our lives. That calling requires us to carry our cross and follow Jesus above all else. There is immense value in being a child of the King, and we will continue to fight against the one who would have us believe worldly gain is the purpose of our time on earth. Do not be fooled—your soul and what you do with the time and resources you steward matter on an eternal scale.

SCRIPTURE FOCUS

MARK 8:36

"For what does it profit a
man to gain the whole
world and forfeit his
soul?"

CHAPTER 6

THE VALUE OF A SOUL

THE STEWARDING OF A TALENT

Serving others breaks you free from the shackles
of self and self-absorption that choke out the joy
of living.

— JAMES C. HUNTER

In 2006, Jamye and I were newlyweds living in Johnson City, Tennessee. She grew up Baptist and I grew up Presbyterian, so we visited several churches across the denominational spectrum searching for the one that would blend our preferences. We tried both traditional and contemporary services, stained glass sanctuaries, large gymnasiums, and even a church that served coffee and donuts as we walked through the front door. Each one had wonderful people and its own unique flare for the gospel, but it took time to find the church that felt like home.

Eventually, we found the right church for the two of us and became regulars on Sundays. One morning, a young woman walked into the sanctuary wearing a Guns N' Roses tee shirt. It is embarrassing to admit, but I reacted as I imagine the Pharisees did when Jesus was preaching in the temple. I completely looked past who this woman was and judged her based on my own bias without giving her a chance to defend herself. I didn't know who she was or how she had gotten to church that day, but I couldn't see any reason as to why someone would think it was appropriate to wear a Guns N' Roses shirt in church.

I have no idea if she saw my face in the crowd. I hope she didn't, because I hate to think of what my facial expressions would have conveyed. I was so wrapped up in this idea that Sunday service was a time to wear your Sunday best and look the part that I didn't see the person standing before me in need. I was later told she and her husband had hit hard times and had lost nearly everything.

I have thought about that morning countless times and how my view of that woman has changed. I have met plenty of people who go to church, quote scripture, and serve on numerous committees, but are never seen in circles outside their church community. She appeared to me as an outsider that day, but the truth is, she showed tremendous courage and strength. She was there despite what clothes she had to wear to a church where most people would expect to find suits and ties.

She was no different than you and me. She needed God's love, a body of believers to be a part of her life, and a savior to provide all the things this world tried to take from her. Nothing in that moment made her soul any less valuable than mine, and her eternity will last just as long.

Weight of a Talent

In 2022, my entire mindset around money and financial discipline as it relates to faith began to change. A great friend and spiritual mentor suggested that one of the problems with the western Church is that it has not figured out how to leverage capitalism for kingdom causes. As you read the word "capitalism," avoid the urge to jump into a political party line. This is not about politics; it's about our view of money and how to use it as a resource for advancing the kingdom.

Within months of him saying this to me, another friend I had only recently met began to speak about the amount of wealth we have in the western church. There is more financial wealth in our churches than at any other time in history, and if we believe our money is God's money, then what are we doing with our resources to take the gospel to the ends of the earth?

These conversations make me think of the teaching of Jesus in Matthew 25:14-30, commonly known as "The Parable of the Talents." In this parable, Jesus tells of a man going on a journey who gathers his servants and entrusts them to be good stewards of his property until he returns. As we unpack what the servants did with the talents they were given, we need to discuss the term "talent". Many will teach this parable explaining that "talents" represent natural abilities. Others will point to the Greek translation of the word where "talent" is a weight of measure valued at twenty years of labor wages. I don't know that either should be considered right or wrong, simply because the parable is ultimately teaching about stewardship, and the two go hand-in-hand.

We will see that money and ability are much more than a means of personal security. They are tools to spread the gospel and reach the unreached, and this parable is all about our stewardship of resources for the Kingdom until Jesus returns. The Greek word for stewardship is "oikonomos," which is where we get the word "economy." Faithful stewardship begins in our homes and moves outward as we grow in our kingdom building.

To the first servant, the master gave five talents, to the second he gave two talents, and to the third he gave a single talent, "each according to his ability" (Mathew 25:15). The servant who received five talents traded with them and doubled his master's property. The second servant also doubled his talents from two to four. The third servant buried his talent in the ground and gained no more. When their master returned, he brought them into his presence to settle his accounts. The first servant reported that he doubled what his master had given him, and the second servant did the same. To both of them, the master replies "Well done, good and faithful servant. You have been faithful over a little; I will set you over much. Enter into the joy of your master!" (Matthew 25:21, 23).

When the last servant stepped up, he told the master he had been afraid and buried his one talent in the ground. The master replied very differently to this servant and insisted that he ought to have invested the money in the bank so he could have at least made interest. He took the talent from the servant and gave it to the one who had multiplied the five talents into ten.

The parable closes with the master saying, "For to everyone who has will more be given, and he will have an abundance. But from the one who has not, even what he has will be taken away. And cast the worthless servant into the outer darkness. In that place there will be weeping and gnashing of teeth" (Matthew 25:29-30).

Like these servants, we have received our own abilities and finances with the God-given authority to decide how they are to be used for the kingdom. We are stewards of God's resources, and there will be a day when we will give an account as to how they were invested. To hear God say, "well done good and faithful servant" will be so much sweeter than, "you wicked and slothful servant."

If my friends were accurate in their statements and we have more resources than ever in the church, all of it belonging to God, then the weight of our decisions in our stewardship carries an eternal consequence. If there are billions of people yet to hear the gospel, then how could we not consider the way we use our abilities and finances to reach them?

Ultimately, the stewardship of these talents is not for our gain, but for the gain of God's kingdom. Therefore, the weight of a talent is enormous for both ourselves as well as those who may be impacted by it in a way that brings them to Christ.

A Work Prayer

I remember working at my home office in September of 2012, wondering if I had what it took to be successful in a relatively new sales role. I had been in that position for eighteen months after moving from the healthcare industry into an IT startup where I sold various technologies. I had stood on stages receiving national awards in healthcare, but for some reason I felt like I couldn't spell "IT." The self-doubt was horrible, and I made a commitment to Jamye that if I didn't quickly figure out how to support us in that role, I would be looking for a new job.

That particular Friday afternoon, I was waiting for a final purchase order to close out our quarter. All eyes were on me, as this was a substantial project that would majorly impact our business. As the hours passed, I began to lose hope that I would see any progress before the client left work for the day. In my despair, I did something I had never done before. I got on my knees and prayed to God about my business.

My prayer was not that God would somehow miraculously close the deal. I didn't want to look at Him like a genie, but I needed Him to keep me from imploding if the deal didn't come through. I was in a position where I had done everything within my power to put my company in the best possible position to win the project, and all I could do was wait and pray.

I prayed, but wasn't sure if God listened to prayers about business. Turns out, He does. Five o'clock came and went, and as I began to shut down my office, an email came through at nearly 5:30 that included the formal purchase order. I froze and then called Jamye to tell her I had done it! I don't believe God heard my prayer and decided to force the hand of someone to send a purchase order, but I do believe God heard my prayer and allowed me to sit in the unknown, leaning on Him for comfort when I could not produce an outcome for myself. That was such a powerful moment.

Fast forward a few years, and I began to produce at a higher level than I ever had. Now, I grew up in a modest house. We were not poor, but there wasn't a lot of extravagance. We had plenty and my childhood was phenomenal, but I had never experienced being in a position where money flowed and I could buy nearly anything I wanted. That feeling of standing on stage again with my newfound success and a growing income was intoxicating. I wanted more of both.

One evening I was speaking with another salesman on our team who is one of the greatest producers I've ever met. We were talking about a specific project and I was asking how he would handle a few things when I said something that triggered a response that politely forced me to face how I was looking at my business, my clients, and my finances. He said, "When's the last time you worried more about your customer than your wallet?"

That question stung, and he was right to ask. I had gotten carried away in my success and forgot what was most important. I had begun to take my customers for granted, and I was viewing my sales platform as a way to improve my life rather than a platform to share the gospel and be a witness. I was being a poor steward of what had been given to me.

VALUE OF A SOUL

"And calling the crowd to him with his disciples, he said to them, 'If anyone would come after me, let him deny himself and take up his cross and follow me. For whoever would save his life will lose it, but whoever loses his life for my sake and the gospel's will save it. For what does it profit a man to gain the whole world and forfeit his soul?'" (Mark 8:34-36).

As Jesus is addressing a crowd and the disciples, He asserts that anyone who would follow Him will have to deny himself and bear his cross. He is telling them that a life genuinely dedicated to serving Him comes with a cost, and that cost is complete surrender. There is no middle ground - you cannot be a disciple of Jesus and put your comforts, finances, security, or worldly acceptance above His will for your life, even unto death. We will all die a physical death, but that doesn't mean we will necessarily be martyred if we follow Jesus. That is not the guaranteed outcome Jesus is referencing. There is however a spiritual death we must experience, and that is dying to our own ambitions and self-seeking desires that don't align with God's desires.

We cannot save ourselves, and Jesus has already

atoned for our sins on the cross to pay our ransom. Why then do we continue to seek approval and security from this world? It has no saving power. In fact, not only can the world not save us, it doesn't want to! Only the cross has that power, and we owe everything to Him.

Imagine your life is a bank, and the world makes deposits into your bank for eighty years. You have millions of dollars, own many homes, and can purchase anything you desire—you have power and prestige, but no relationship with Jesus. With all that the world deposited into your account, you would still be eternally bankrupt. The world can give you everything except salvation through Jesus Christ. That is what it means to gain the whole world and yet forfeit your soul. The soul is infinitely valuable and eternally important to our Lord.

The harsh reality is so many people will do this very thing, they will forfeit their souls for a life of earthly treasure and pleasure. I'm not just talking about people who have never heard the name of Jesus, I'm talking about people who claim to follow Him as well.

THE RICH YOUNG RULER

Not everyone who met Jesus was eager and willing to leave their possessions in order to follow Him. We know the same is true today - people will encounter Jesus but refuse to give up authority over their lives. In Mark 10, we meet one of these individuals in a story commonly called "The Rich Young Ruler."

This young man approaches Jesus asking what he must do to inherit eternal life. Jesus begins to speak with him about the commandments, to which the young man replies he has kept all of them since his youth. At this point, I imagine the man must have felt rather positive about his odds. That's when Jesus, looking upon him with love, told the young man to do something he found far too difficult.

"And Jesus, looking at him, loved him, and said to him, 'You lack one thing: go, sell all that you have and give to the poor, and you will have treasure in heaven; and come, follow me'" (Mark 10:21).

I want you to see two very important truths from Jesus in this exchange. First, Jesus loved this young man who was lost. Reading the text, we see that He was not flippant or annoyed by the young man seeking wisdom for how to gain eternal life. He saw him as someone in need of a savior and felt compassion toward him. Second, Jesus was not insinuating that in order to follow Him any of us, including the young man, would have to live in poverty or not have any kind of wealth. Salvation is not based on wealth, or lack thereof, but is based on the heart. Earthly possessions cannot possess the heart if we are to follow Jesus.

"Disheartened by the saying, he went away sorrowful, for he had great possessions" (Mark 10:22).

The young man said he had kept the commandments, but in truth, he was in love with possessions from which he felt he could not part. Jesus didn't say to throw them into the sea; He said to sell everything and give to the poor, but generosity to the less fortunate was not an option for this young man.

As discussed previously, money can become a great inhibitor for young people who would like to enter into traditional missionary work because they often don't have much of it and typically accumulate debt from school. On the other end of the spectrum, there are plenty of working adults who have a great amount of money, yet they hold it so tight and find value and security through it rather than through Jesus.

"No one can serve two masters, for either he will hate the one and love the other, or he will be devoted to the one and despise the other. You cannot serve God and money" (Matthew 6:24).

Not only did the rich young ruler forfeit heaven for temporary possessions and wealth, he never understood the value of a soul or the weight of a talent. A man of his stature and financial position would've had a great opportunity to reach others with the gospel, but he squandered that opportunity through self-absorption. This story has taught me the importance of putting our trust in things that are eternal rather than things that will pass away with time.

Reflection

IF YOU HAVE EVER FLOWN COMMERCIALLY,
you know before takeoff there is a safety briefing
where procedures of what to do in case of an emergency are reviewed. As the flight attendants stand
before you giving instructions, you will hear something to the effect of "secure your mask before
assisting others." The mask is there to provide the
necessary oxygen you need in the event the cabin
loses air pressure. It is no different as we prepare to
go into the world to share the gospel.

As the pressures of this world try to squeeze
the air from our lungs, we need to secure our
masks in order to help those around us. We do that
by filling our hearts with God's word, surrounding
ourselves with those who will sharpen us, and
growing in relationship with Him. If you're
thinking those things can be challenging, I understand. Our human nature wants to rebel, and just
because we have accepted Christ as Lord does not
mean sin isn't trying to enter into our lives. Even
so, we must fight against those attacks and finish
the task at hand.

It is imperative we understand the value of a
soul, both ours and others, and recognize the
eternal weight of a talent. We must return to our

oxygen masks when our lungs are empty so that we can turn to our left and right to help those around us. Fill your lungs, and as you are going, intentionally invest into the lives of those you encounter so that they will recognize the value of their soul and exercise wisdom in the use of their talents.

"Then I heard the voice
of the Lord, saying,
'Whom shall I send, and
who will go for Us?'
Then I said, 'Here am I.
Send me!'"

CHAPTER 7

SEND ME

RESPONDING TO GOD'S CALL

Courage is contagious. When a brave man takes
a stand, the spines of others are stiffened.

— BILLY GRAHAM

I t frustrates me when I hear someone calling
work a four-letter word. We often see work
as an obstacle rather than an opportunity. It
is the double-edged sword that keeps our mort-
gages paid and food on our tables, but also stands
between us and retirement or enjoying hobbies
outside the office. We complain about what we
have to do and how busy we are to finish the tasks
and responsibilities assigned to us.

Rarely are we encouraged to see work as a gift

in a world that focuses on self-advancement and satisfaction. Everywhere you look, someone has a program to grow your bank account while you work less and play more. The idea sounds great, but unless that financial freedom enables you to do more kingdom-building activities and enhance the lives of your family, it's only temporary at best.

I love our churches, but how many of our pastors are being taught in seminaries how to show their congregations that their work outside the church matters and can be God-honoring? Do American congregations hear that they can magnify God as they put their gifts, skills, and talents into practice? Or do we only preach about work and business as part of a prosperity gospel?

We have missed what was ordained in the original intent of work, and as a result, it has become little more than something we have to do to survive. God's design for work was meant to be so much more, and because we live in a fallen world, the value we place on our work has turned from God-glorifying to self-indulging.

Work has become the defining component of one's identity in our culture. Think about it for a moment—when you introduce yourself to someone in almost any setting, how many times do you say something like, "My name is Paul, and I'm an attorney," or, "I'm Mary, and I'm in sales."

What about the way you spend your time? Do you miss special events—your child's ballgame or dinner a few nights each week—in order to stay in the office just a *little* longer so you can finish that proposal, meet that client for happy hour, or bill your customer for a little more of your time?

I understand there are seasons in our work where we may need to pour extra time into what we do. There will always be exceptions, but missing your life because you choose work in its place is not an exception–it's a destructive behavior that leads to broken relationships and exhausted minds and bodies.

I once read an article claiming 92% of men had never heard a sermon about work. I know statistics can be bent to support one opinion or another, but let's assume for a moment that data point is accurate. If it's true, the correlation between faith and work hardly exists for the men sitting in the pews of our churches. If that many men have not heard a sermon about work, what percentage of women would say the same?

Just as God has been removed from so many institutions in this world, such as our schools and in government, He has also been removed from the workplace in the name of equality and inclusion. We hear about the separation of church and state, and this concept carries into corporations of all sizes. Speaking about politics and religion is unacceptable, yet we often see other agendas and non-Christian ideologies highlighted and promoted to employees in the name of diversity. It's very ironic that God's creation is so intentionally diverse, yet it has been twisted into a tool used against us to divide and polarize the very people called to love one another in His name.

Herein lies the problem: Christians are called to run toward those who need to hear the name of Jesus. Churches don't exist to be spiritual country clubs for like-minded believers who never step outside the doors of their sanctuaries. At the same time, we know that many people will never darken the door of a church if they are not welcomed in by those who already believe.

What are we to do? Where do those of us not called to be pastors and missionaries go to share our faith with an unbelieving world? The answer is the very businesses and organizations where we spend our day-to-day lives.

A corporate chaplain friend of mine said that his organization works alongside several local businesses comprised of nearly eight-hundred employees. In the past two years, he has attended more than forty funerals for these employees and their families. In addition, the families of those employees have experienced roughly sixty suicides in this short period of time.

Our businesses are full of people that need to hear that God knows their pains and hurts, and He cares about them and their work. We spend so much of our lives working, why would we not want to lean into the lives of others and share the gospel? People are hurting and we are already there with them - let's make it count for more than our own personal gain.

APPLICATION

You may feel intimidated, awkward, or even inadequate when you consider what it means to integrate your faith with your work. Just know that you don't have to be a theologian or full-time ministry worker to talk with others about God. Don't be afraid to make mistakes; they're inevitable. You're human, so allow yourself room for grace and growth. You know how He has impacted your life, and that's the perfect place to start.

Ask God to Make You Aware of Others & Lead You

I was once told the world sees Christians as boring, irrelevant hypocrites who pretend to care about people but in truth only want their money. What would happen if we asked God to guide our steps and lead us to these people so that we can show them something different?

I often take my son Wyatt to school in the mornings, and we say a brief prayer as we pull into the parking lot. I try to always say something to the effect of, "Father God, thank you for this day. Thank you for your love, mercy, and grace. Thank you that we have another day to learn and grow at school, and please make us aware of those around us who need to know who you are. Guide us, and give us an opportunity to speak with them today." It's simple, and I trust God to answer as Wyatt learns how to speak with and hear from God.

A friend of mine is a business owner who regularly invites God into his meetings with clients and teammates. He told me he prays each morning, "Lord put me in the right place, at the right time, with the right people, doing the right thing. Make it clear, and kick me in the rear. Amen!" I love his prayer!

Share Your Faith & Learn From Others

When I took my few classes in seminary, I had an assignment that I wasn't sure I could complete. The professor asked us to meet with someone of another faith and culture in order to share what we believe, and also ask them to share with us their beliefs. I reached out to a coworker and explained that I had an assignment for seminary and asked if he would be willing to speak with me.

I explained the details and assured him he was not a project, but I needed to complete the assignment in order to pass. He asked me if I was trying to convert him. I said absolutely not, explained that I knew he was a Muslim and genuinely wanted to have a conversation with him, and that this assignment forced the opportunity to approach him. He went silent for a moment on the other end of the phone before asking if I was interested in becoming Hindu, Muslim, or Buddhist. I responded that I was not interested, and he said, "perfect, let's talk!"

We spent hours in conversation, and I learned so much about him on both a personal and spiritual level. Our discussions were honest and raw, as we agreed to not withhold anything for the sake of being politically correct. We covered any topic you could imagine from a theological perspective, and there were a few times it was difficult when we had to agree to disagree. We spoke of Heaven and how to get there. That was the most uncomfortable conversation I may have ever had, but we both approached it with grace and kindness.

Go Where the People Are

A few years into my technology sales career, I spent time with a VP-level financial lender at a company event. As we sat down at the bar, we had one of the most amazing conversations about God, family, and work. I had always been told not to get drunk, but never knew I could drink a bourbon while talking with someone about Jesus. In no way am I condoning drunkenness, but I think sometimes we must go where people are in order to share the gospel. Before that event, I did not know this man was a Christian. To this day, this gentleman is one of the most respected businessmen I have ever met and does so much for the Kingdom of God. That was one of the best bourbons I've ever had.

In John 5, Jesus visits the healing pool at Bethesda. This healing pool was surrounded by people who were blind, lame, and paralyzed. They would have been considered outcasts, shunned by society, but at the healing pool, they were all on equal ground in their desperate search for healing and restoration. It's a scene that serves as a great reminder–everyone wants somewhere they can belong.

Jesus sees a man who had been unable to walk for thirty-eight years, and asks him, "Do you want to be healed?" (John 5:6). The people at the pool believed that an angel would stir the waters, and the first person to enter the pool would be healed. Unable to walk, the man could never be the first to enter the water. Jesus knew this and said "'Get up! Pick up your mat and walk.' At once the man was cured; he picked up his mat and walked" (John 5:8).

The healing of the man who was lame for nearly four decades should have been a day of cele-bration, but the religious people who saw the man walking about were upset that Jesus had healed this man on the Sabbath. Their response was ludicrous, but so was the idea that Jesus would spend time with the sick and the outcasts. Go where the people are!

Spend Time in Worship

I don't have a fear of public speaking, but singing in public terrifies me. I have sung at church a number of times, even though I don't have the most incredible voice. I do it because it forces me to step outside my comfort zone and it's a form of worship. My son Wyatt and I sang a song last year by Zack Williams titled "Heaven Help Me." He loved it and I am so proud of him for standing onstage in front of nearly a hundred people.

Singing is a form of worship, but so are other things like reading scripture, prayer, and even work! In the book of Genesis, Adam and Eve are placed in the Garden of Eden as its caretakers. My grandfather, who has farmed most of his life, will tell you that the oldest profession in the world is farming thanks to Adam and Eve.

A pastor friend of mine pointed out that Adam and Eve could work before they could even die. Think about that for a minute–before God removed them from the garden for disobeying His command, death was not a concern, but working the garden was one of the tasks they'd been given.

"The Lord God took the man and put him in the Garden of Eden to work it and take care of it . . . The Lord God said, 'It is not good for the man to

be alone. I will make a helper suitable for him'"
(Genesis 4:15,18).

Take Action & Don't Focus On the Results

When I was young, my parents gave me a Bible
and wrote "Isaiah 41:10" inside the front cover.
The verse reads "fear not, for I am with you; be not
dismayed, for I am your God; I will strengthen
you, I will help you, I will uphold you with my
righteous right hand." I can't tell you how many
times I've thought of that verse over the years when
I'm afraid of making a mistake or am uncertain in a
situation. Know that God is faithful to keep His
promises and will stand beside you regardless of
what may come.

The cross looks like a total failure to the
world, and we appear to be religious lunatics.
There are times when we will be greeted as such,
and that's okay. "You believe that there is one
God. Good! Even the demons believe that—and
shudder" (James 2:19). We are called not only to
believe in Jesus but also to take action in sharing
our faith with others. That can be small acts of
kindness, saying the blessing at a meal, asking to
pray for someone, or inviting a friend to church.
Small steps of faith usher in new opportunities

over time to grow in your ability to boldly share the gospel.

I hate when people make a game out of "winning souls" for Jesus. I understand that we want people to come to Jesus, but it's not some kind of spiritual trophy to be placed on our mantle. Faith can be a very personal part of someone's life, and when we use language like that, it drives them away. It looks like a spiritual game and not like an eternal decision with real consequences. Don't do it. Instead, plant a seed of faith and allow room for God to do what He does.

PLANTING SEEDS OF FAITH

"If I tell you a chicken can pull a plow, hook him up!" My grandfather said this to me hundreds of times growing up. It didn't matter if we were working on his old Ford tractor in the middle of a field, heading down a two-lane highway with a load of corn, feeding livestock, or eating dinner around that old table in the farmhouse dining room. When he felt the need to remind me of a chicken's unexplainable ability to pull a plow, he made sure to do so. I never questioned him. The truth is, I figured he knew something about chickens I just had not yet learned. To this day, I will not bet against him on whether or not it is possible.

I imagine this was my grandfather's way of asking me to trust him beyond what I had already determined to be plausible. While the farm was a world of adventure for a young boy, I had no idea what it took for my grandfather and uncle to manage it.

As a child, I saw the farm through the eyes of a child. I rode tractors while plowing fields, fed animals early in the morning, watched my grandfather and uncle work on equipment, and delivered livestock and produce to the farmer's market. I only recognized these events for what they were in those moments. At the same time, I only saw my grandfather as a farmer even though he was an entrepreneur running his own business.

Growing up, I would visit the farm at various times of the year, so I would often either see the planting season or the harvest, but rarely would I witness both. Maybe that's why I remain so impressed that a tiny seed planted in fertile ground can grow into something both wonderful and useful.

My grandfather and uncle will tell you that a lot of work goes into planting, and once the seed is in the ground there is only so much they can do as they wait for the seed to sprout from the earth. There is a period of time when they must trust that a transformation is happening beneath the soil.

Planting seeds of faith is not all that different. Some people will plant seeds, others will water, and yet others will harvest. We all have a role to play in the spreading of God's word, and it all begins with planting that little seed that has the power to grow into something beautiful.

SEND ME

We have witnessed God's hand on Esther's life to become a kingdom builder "for such a time as this." As sons and daughters of the King, we too are royalty with God-given authority to be kingdom builders.

The prodigal son and his father proved God's love for His children in spite of their mistakes, reminding us that we are never too far from His love.

David, the shepherd boy who became king, slayed the giant Goliath with only his sling and a stone. He trusted God would deliver him from the giant and went into battle without reservation.

Genesis and Revelation played like a movie

trailer, showing us both the beginning of creation and the end of time.

Luke's account of the crucifixion presented us with the criminals who were nailed to their crosses at Jesus' side. While one only cared to save himself in the physical, the other trusted Jesus to save him spiritually and found salvation in his final moments.

Jesus rose from the grave and left us with a command to "make disciples of all nations, baptizing them in the name of the Father and of the Son and of the Holy Spirit" (Matthew 28:19).

Simon became Simon Peter and was no longer a fisherman, but a fisher of men.

Saul was a great adversary of God's people and became their greatest champion.

Three servants and their master demonstrated the weight of a talent and the importance of properly stewarding all we are given. Jesus will return one day, and we will be held accountable for what we did with the talents in our possession.

A rich young ruler asked Jesus what he must do to inherit eternal life, only to hear a response that left him disheartened and unable to let go of his possessions. His great wealth became a greater stumbling block. He could not carry the weight of a talent and did not understand the value of a soul.

We observed Isaiah's encounter with God and the six-winged seraphim. He was in the temple of the Lord and it was filled with smoke. The doorposts and thresholds shook, and the seraphim were shouting "Holy, holy, holy is the LORD Almighty." A terrified Isaiah fell to his knees in the presence of the King awaiting judgment. To his surprise, he was spared and experienced spiritual cleansing as a burning coal was placed against his lips.

We now come full circle with Isaiah as he responds to God's calling: "Then I heard the voice of the Lord, saying, 'Whom shall I send, and who will go for Us?' Then I said, 'Here am I. Send me!'" (Isaiah 6:8 NASB).

In eight short verses, Isaiah goes from fearing for his life to receiving grace and sanctification, to eagerly volunteering to be a messenger for the Lord. His entire reason for living changed in these moments as he found himself fully trusting God before he even knew what message he would be delivering. Without hesitation, he made himself available to God's service, raising his hand and exclaiming, "Here am I. Send Me!"

God still calls us into His service thousands of years after He called Isaiah. It is a massive responsibility and beautiful opportunity to serve the God of the universe who wants to see the people of this world come to salvation. When called upon, before we even know what God is going to require of us, I pray we will raise our hands and shout like Isaiah, "Here am I. Send Me!"

ALWAYS FAITHFUL

I wrote about my father-in-law Eddie earlier in this book and how we recently celebrated his retirement from a distinguished sales career in December of 2022. A month after I wrote that chapter, Eddie passed away unexpectedly, and his funeral was held on February 18, 2023. Hundreds of people came to remember and celebrate his life. Our small country church sanctuary has capacity for roughly three hundred people, and I have never seen it so full. When the pews had no more space available, chairs were brought in, and when we ran out of chairs, a number of folks had to stand along the back wall.

I met many people for the first time that day, with Eddie being the common thread between us. In attendance were a number of cousins, neighbors, customers, and work colleagues. There were several people who had known Eddie since the mid-80s when they worked together. Nearly forty years later, they came to tell his family how much he meant to them and the impact he had on their lives.

Four of us spoke during the funeral service, sharing personal stories and reflections. The first speaker was Bill, a county administrator in South Carolina who grew up a few houses down from my in-laws. My wife considers Bill to be her big brother, and he called Eddie "Daddy Eddie" growing up.

The second gentleman, Rick, grew up with four brothers in his home, and Eddie became a "sixth son" to his parents in high school. Rick shared four or five stories that had everyone in tears from laughing, and he spoke of how Eddie would go out of his way to include him in trips and everyday activities like going to the store and running errands.

The third person to speak was one of Eddie's longtime surveying clients, Mark. In the mid-90s, Eddie cold-called Mark and before he walked out the door, Mark gave him a chance to quote an item they needed. Eddie got his business and continued earning it over a 25-year relationship. Mark made sure everyone in the church knew Eddie was not just a salesman but a friend, and someone he relied on to help him be successful.

Eddie did so much to help his clients that the South Carolina Association of Land Surveyors awarded him a Lifetime Service Award and a scholarship is being created in his name. His impact and service to the business community were exceptional and uncommon.

I spoke last at the funeral from the unique position as Eddie's only son-in-law. I shared stories about dating Jamye and how Eddie trusted me with his daughter's heart. I shared about the time we got sick deep sea fishing and how if Jamye hadn't been sick, Eddie would have left me out there with no hope of going back to shore early. I shared about asking Eddie for his blessing to marry Jamye over breakfast one morning, and how he asked me if I was sure. Our love for Jamye brought us together in a unique relationship, and I had the opportunity to see Eddie from several different perspectives: as a husband, father, grandfather, businessman, servant leader, and man of God.

Through the stories shared that day, and the countless people who reached out with their condolences, Eddie was described as a man who was steady, confident, and loved Jesus. He lived his faith through his vocation. His work was his mission field. He was the same guy Monday through Saturday that he was on Sunday morning.

Eddie was also a Marine, and our pastor reminded us that the Marine Corps motto is "Semper Fidelis" which translates to "Always Faithful." That's what Eddie was in all areas of his life, including his work.

In the end, Eddie gave me a great gift in witnessing his example of how to be on mission with God through our work. I had not fully recognized it during his life, and I imagine that's because he wasn't a flashy or boastful person. His actions were louder than words. For twenty-three years I saw him through the lens of a son-in-law, but through the celebration of his life, I can now see him as a man who pointed others to Christ through his work.

Reflection

He who knows no bounds
Is the only one in whom eternal life can be found
The world fights for your soul, ever nipping at
your heel
But don't lose heart, He understands what you feel
Do not believe the lie that you are to be left on
your own
For you have been granted a warrior's heart, given
from His throne
So do not stop, move forward lest your heart
becomes still
For He has won the victory over him who comes
only to kill
Take your stand, lift your sword with an anthem
raised
And speak His name from here into every place
In the darkness of the fight, chained hearts are
set free
Shouting to the Lord, Here am I, Send Me!

— EVANS DUREN

Acknowledgments

Thank you, Lord, for your unending love, mercy, and grace. Thank you for the tension that first stirred my heart so many years ago. Thank you for your patience, as well as your prodding. Thank you for allowing me to be a vessel. I pray you are pleased.

Thank you to Jamye, Clark, and Wyatt for lifting me up when I am down. Thank you for making me want to fight through trying times so that I may become the man God has called me to be for our family and this world. Thank you for loving all of me, and for the opportunity to love you in return.

Thank you Rene, Robert, and Jamye for your blessing to share a small portion of Eddie's story with the world. I promise to share it with many more along my way.

Thank you to my parents and brothers who shaped and molded me early in my life. No matter what may come, I will forever be grateful for our time under one roof together. I love each of you, thank you.

To my friends and mentors, thank you for your encouragement and unwavering support. I only hope I can repay your kindness and make you feel as unstoppable as you have made me feel.

Thank you to Alex and Will who believed I had a book inside of me that needed to be written. You guys have no idea how much this experience means to me.

Thank you to Trevor and Ben for walking alongside me these past several months through countless edits and revisions. I didn't make it easy. Thank you for leading me through an incredible process.

About the Author

Evans Duren is an award-winning businessman who wants to bridge the divide between the secular and the sacred. He owns The Duren Companies, LLC, a consulting firm that works with individuals and organizations to leverage their unique gifts, skills, and talents to become kingdom builders through their professions. Having worked for Fortune 15 and Technology startups, Evans has seen the impact faith can have on those we encounter daily through our work.

He is married to Jamye, and they have two incredible sons.

www.EvansDuren.com